MW01709759

Father Browne's Images of Tipperary

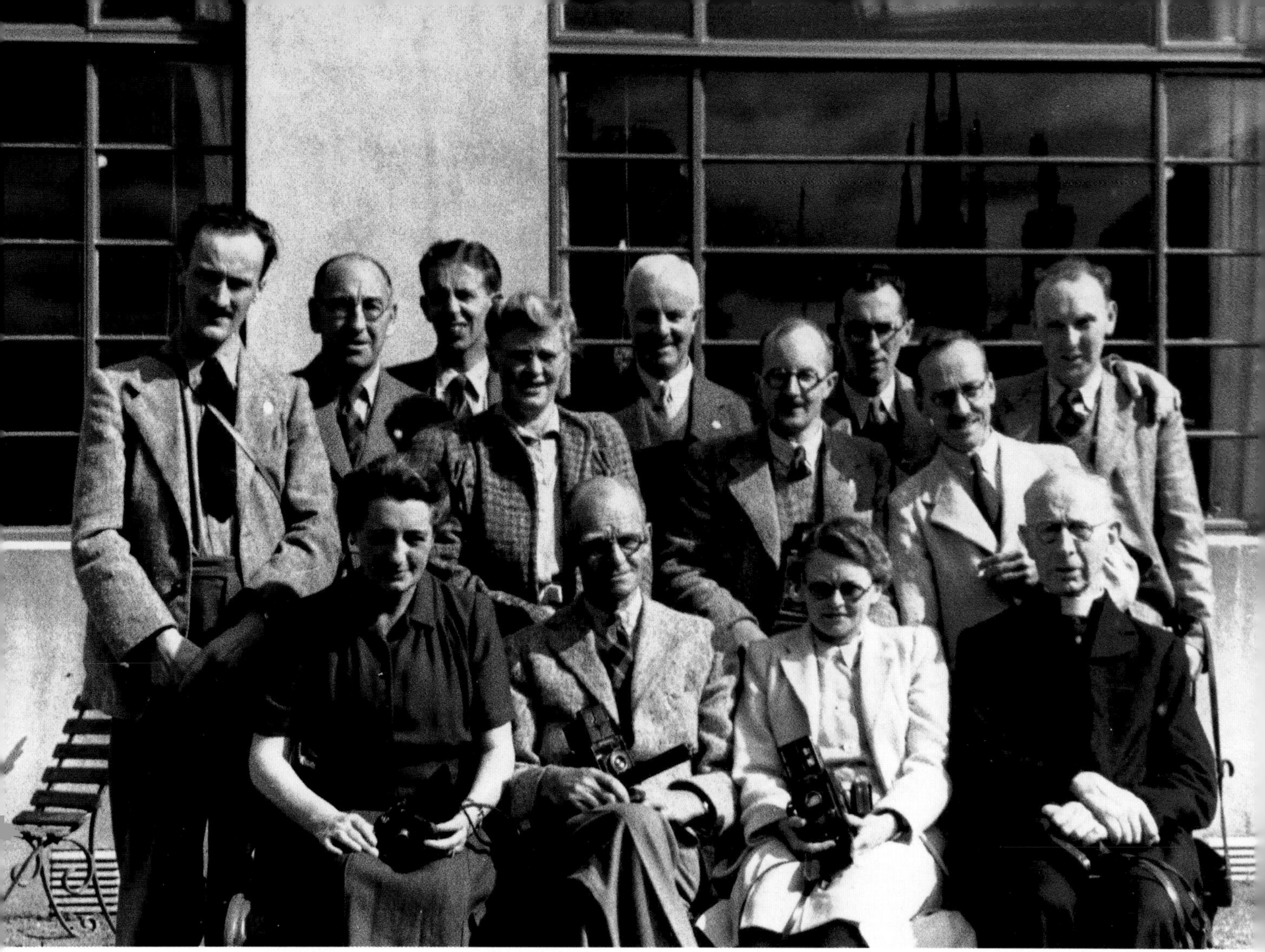

Members of the Photographic Society of Ireland, including Father Browne (seated, on the right), Cashel (1945).

Father Browne's Images of Tipperary

E.E. O'Donnell

WOLFHOUND PRESS

Published in 2001 by
Wolfhound Press
An imprint of Merlin Publishing
16 Upper Pembroke Street, Dublin 2, Ireland
Tel: + 353 1 6764373; Fax: + 353 1 6764368
e-mail: publishing@merlin.ie www: merlin-publishing.com

© 2001 E. E. O'Donnell
Photographs © The Father Browne SJ Collection

All rights reserved. No part of this book may be reproduced or utilised in any form or by any means digital, electronic or mechanical including photography, filming, video recording, photocopying, or by any information storage and retrieval system or shall not, by way of trade or otherwise, be lent, resold or otherwise circulated in any form of binding or cover other than that in which it is published without prior permission in writing from the publisher.

Father Browne prints are available from Davison and Associates
69b Heather Road, Sandyford Industrial Estate, Dublin 18.

British Library Cataloguing in Publication Data
A catalogue record for this book is available from the British Library.

ISBN 0-86327-876-0

5 4 3 2 1

Cover Images: Father Browne SJ Collection
Typesetting and book design: David Houlden
Prints: Davison and Associates
Duotone Separations: Colour Repro Ltd
Printed in the UK by The Bath Press

ALSO BY E.E. O'DONNELL:

Published by Wolfhound Press, Dublin
The Annals of Dublin (1987)
Father Browne's Ireland (1988)
The Genius of Father Browne (1989)
Father Browne's Dublin (1990)
Father Browne: A Life in Pictures (1991)
Father Browne's Cork (1992)
Father Browne's Australia (1995)
Father Browne's England (1996)
Images of Aran (1997)
Father Browne's Titanic Album: A Passenger's Photographs & Memoir (1997)
Father Browne's Ships & Shipping (2000)

Published by The Society of Irish Foresters
Forest Images: Father Browne's Woodland Photographs (1993)

Published by Anatolia Editions, Paris
L'Irlande du père Browne (1996)

Contents

Introduction

It's a long way around County Tipperary if you want to follow in the footsteps of Father Frank Browne. Personally, I put 540 miles on the 'clock' of my car in one three-day period – and I didn't do the half of it. Besides taking photographs in all the major towns of the county, Father Browne visited all of the beauty spots: from Slievenamon to the Glen of Aherlow, from the Devil's Bit to the heights of Galtymore. Of course, he covered such well-known places as Holy Cross Abbey and St Patrick's College, Thurles, but he also photographed places that not even the Post Office knew about – Mooresfort, to name but one. Overall, he took 1,750 pictures of the county.

Father Browne took most of these photographs while directing Parish Missions or giving Convent Retreats. That was his life's work from 1929 until his death in 1960. Readers who are not familiar with his biography might like to read the summary of his life up to 1929 below. Those who want to delve into it further could read my book, *Father Browne: A Life in Pictures*, which was published by Wolfhound Press in 1994.

Frank Browne was born in Cork in 1880. Educated in Athlone, Cork and Dublin, he left school in 1897 and travelled around Europe with his brother – and the new camera presented to him by his uncle, Robert Browne, Bishop of Cloyne. The one-hundred-odd photos he took on this tour were the first in the collection of 42,000 he would go on to take. In September of the same year, he joined the Jesuits. After his two-year noviceship, he attended University College Dublin where he was a classmate of James Joyce. 'Mr Browne the Jesuit' appears in *Finnegans Wake*.

In 1902 Frank was sent to study philosophy in Italy for three years. Based at Chieri, near Turin, he visited many of the art galleries of northern Italy. Experts have pointed out

Frank Browne founded the Camera Club at Belvedere College, Dublin, in 1906. He took a group of the boys to photograph the Rock of Cashel in 1911. The results were published in the college annual, *The Belvederian*, which also had been founded by Frank Browne (1906).

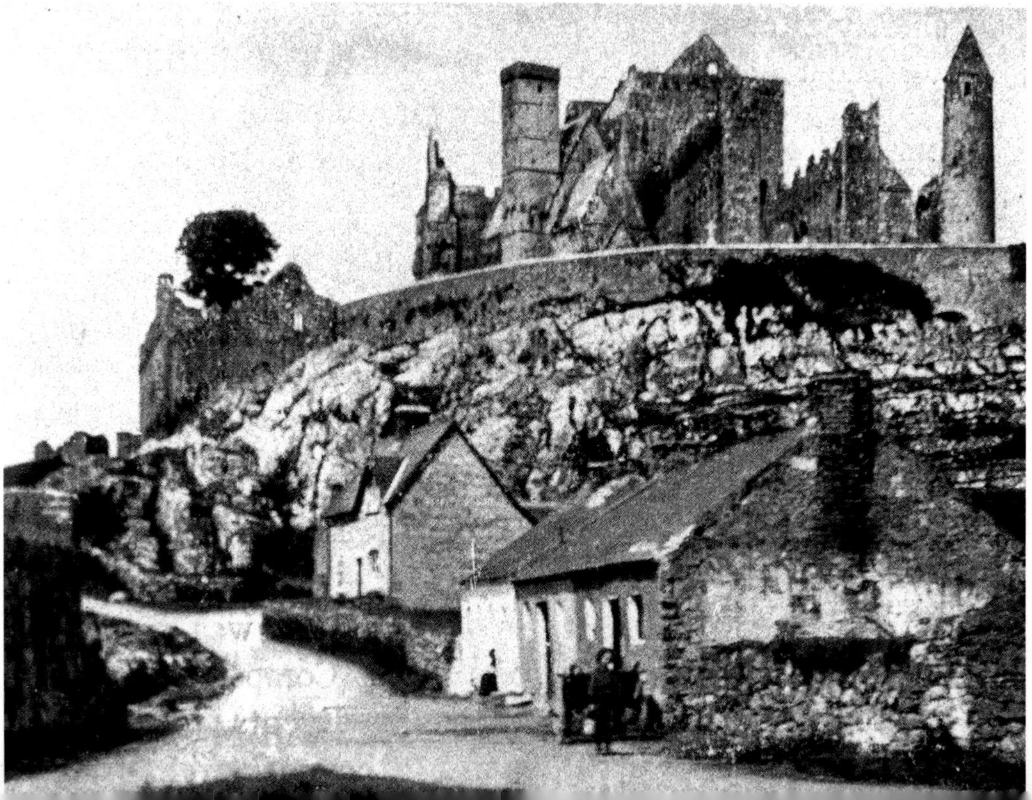

that his studies of the Old Masters during these years added much to his photographic expertise.

In 1906, after a brief stopover at Monte Carlo, Frank returned to Ireland. He taught at Belvedere College in Dublin until 1911. It was during these years that he founded the college annual, the Cycling Club and the Camera Club. The earliest of the County Tipperary pictures in this book were taken during one of the school tours to the Rock of Cashel.

In 1911 Frank began the final stage of his clerical studies, theology, at Milltown Park, Dublin. During his second year there, Uncle Robert sent him a present of a first-class ticket for the maiden voyage of *Titanic* from Southampton to Cherbourg and from Cherbourg to Queenstown (Cobh). When he disembarked at the latter port, unwittingly he was carrying what would be the last surviving photographs of the passengers and crew of the doomed liner.

On 31 July 1913, Frank became 'Father Browne' when he was ordained a priest by the Bishop of Cloyne. On the completion of his theological studies in 1915 he was appointed Chaplain to the Irish Guards. He served in France and Flanders for the duration of World War I and was honoured by the British, French and Belgian governments. After the war, he remained with the Irish Guards on the Rhine until 1920 when he was demobilised.

On returning to Dublin, Father Browne taught at Belvedere College for a further two years before becoming Superior of Gardiner Street Church in Dublin. During his tenure of office there, his health began to deteriorate, owing in part to the mustard-gassing he had suffered in April of 1918. For the good of his lungs he was sent to live in Australia for two years, 1924 and 1925, where he took the photographs that have appeared in book form under the title *Father Browne's Australia*.

From 1926 to 1929 he resumed his work at Gardiner Street and was then appointed to the Retreats and Missions Staff of the Irish Jesuits. This work took him all over the 'home countries' and, as we have noted, all over County Tipperary. Monastic Ireland was a subject dear to Father Browne's heart and he found plenty to photograph in this regard within the borders of the county. The great houses of Ireland were another such subject, but two of these which he ascribed to County Tipperary are in fact not within the borders of the county: Castletown-Cox is in Kilkenny and Gurteen is in Waterford – though in each case by a matter of yards.

Father Browne was still visiting the county in his seventies. Before he died at the age of eighty, he had covered comprehensively every county in Ireland. Books of his photographs of Dublin, Cork and the Aran Islands have already been published. The people of Tipperary will, I hope, be glad to see that they are next on the list. Already they have been treated to exhibitions of Father Browne's work by Ark Life, the assurance subsidiary of Allied Irish Bank which generously subsidises the preservation of the Browne Collection and has contributed to the publication of this book. At AIB banks in Clonmel, Carrick-on-Suir, Tipperary town, Cashel and so on, Ark Life has presented local photographs together with brilliant examples from Father Browne's world-wide collection, including pictures he took in South Africa on his way to Australia, as well as photographs of Ceylon (Sri Lanka) and the Suez Canal through which he travelled on the return journey.

Outside of Ireland, exhibitions of the Browne photographs have been held at venues throughout the United Kingdom, the United States, Belgium, Portugal, Germany and Australia. Two shows that call for particular mention are the 'Images of Ireland' exhibition at the Centre Pompidou in Paris and the *Titanic* exhibition – sponsored by Sony, Kodak and Twentieth Century Fox – which toured six cities in Japan.

On television, RTÉ has twice aired the six-part documentary series on Father Browne's Irish photographs entitled 'The Day before Yesterday': this was the title chosen by Peter Walsh for his exhibition of Father Browne's Dublin pictures at the Guinness Hopstore.

On the publishing front, besides the fourteen titles brought out by Wolfhound Press – which can be found on its website – *L'Irlande du père Browne* was published by Anatolia Editions, Paris, and *Father Browne's Woodland Images* was published by the Society of Irish Foresters.

For help in completing the captions for this book I would like to thank John Walsh, Auctioneer and Local Historian (Templemore), Sisters Aloysius O'Mahony and Bonaventure Tierney of the Presentation Convent (Thurles), Oliver Corbett, Tipperary County Librarian (Carrick-on-Suir), Father Christy O'Dwyer, President, St Patrick's College (Thurles), Mary Crowe, Dundrum House Hotel (Dundrum), J.J. Crowley, Manager, Glanbia Ltd. (Ballypatrick), and Margaret Veale of the Knocklofty House Hotel and Leisure Centre (Clonmel).

Street Scenes

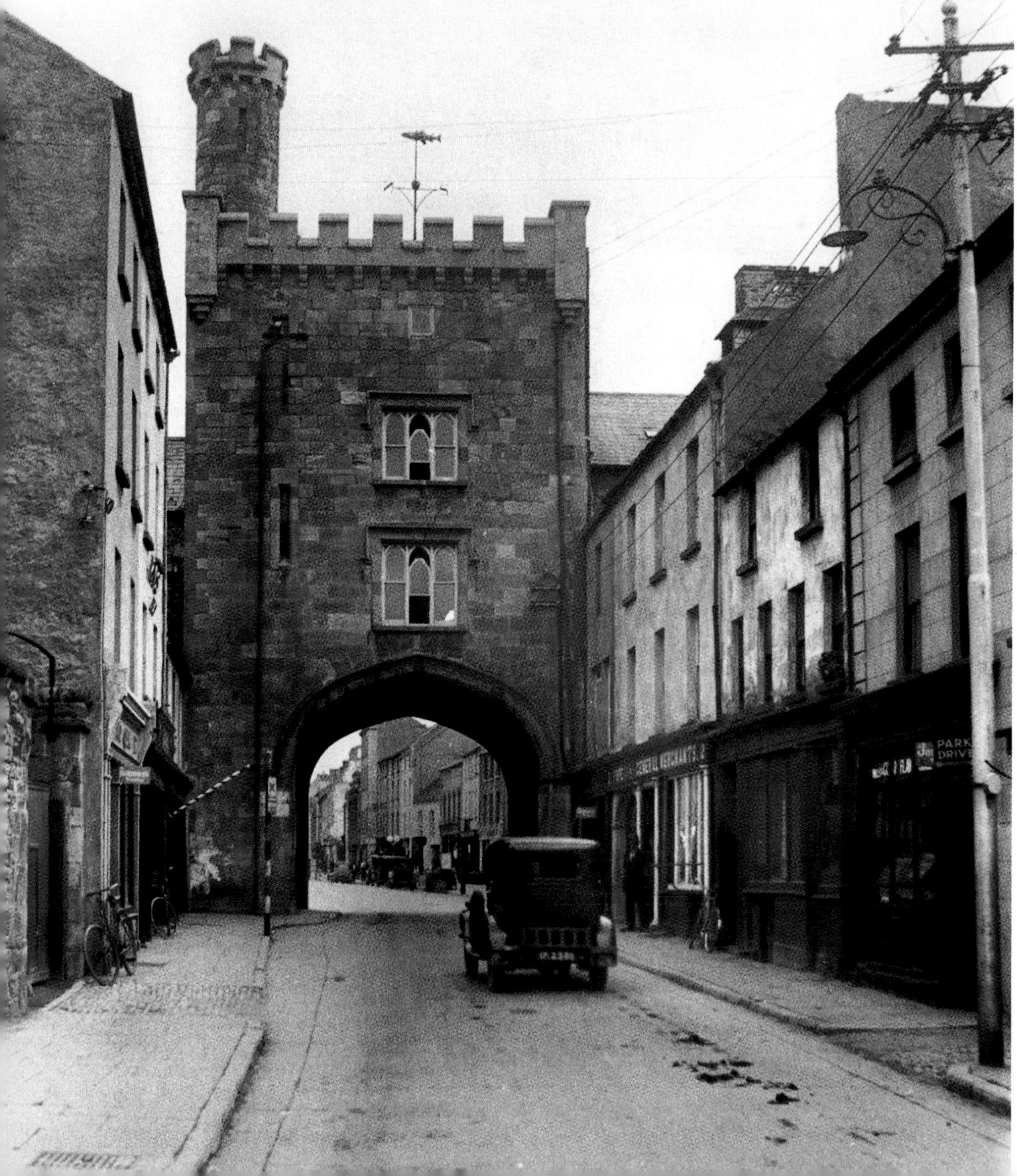

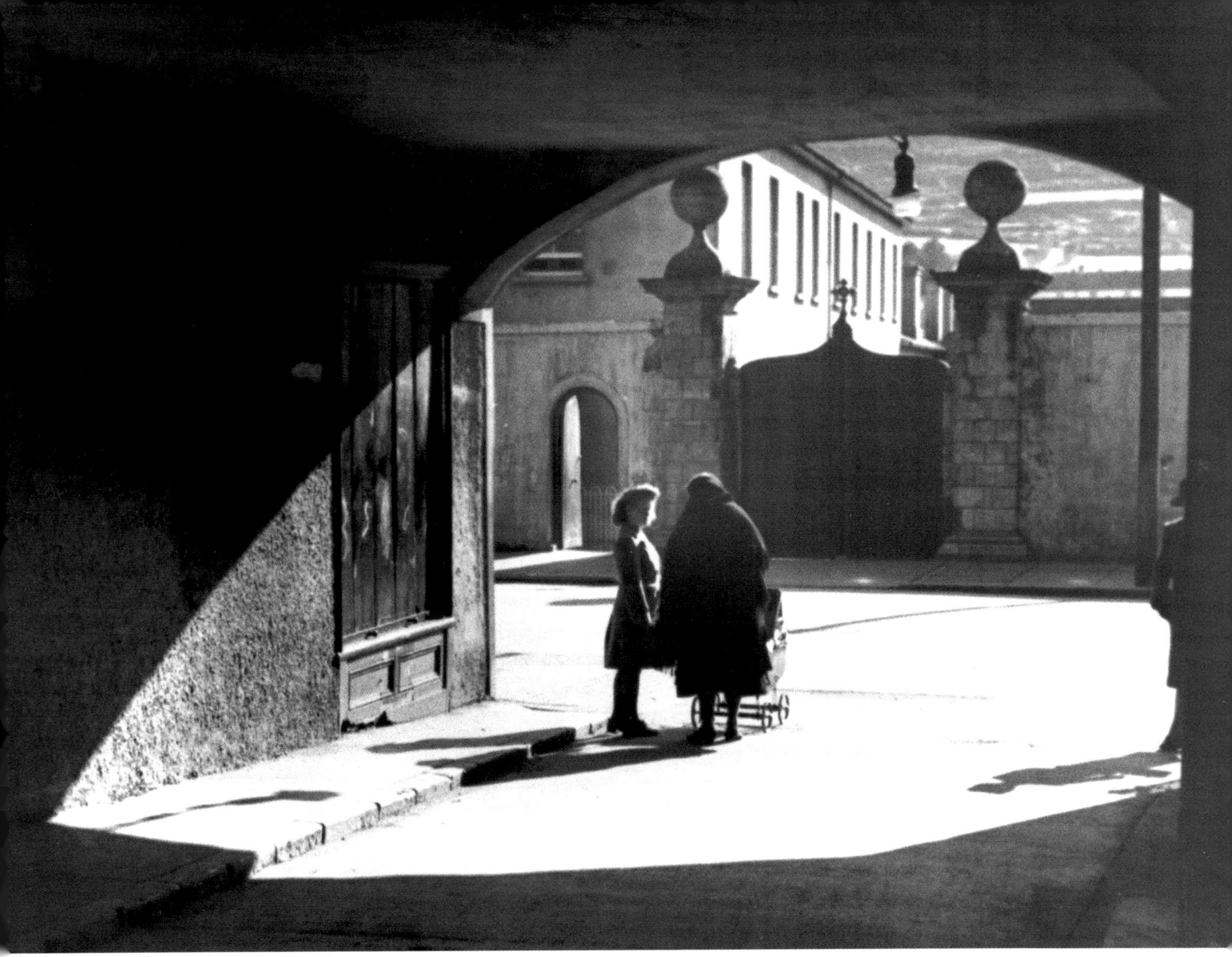

A beautifully framed photograph taken in Chapel Lane, Carrick-on-Suir, in 1944.

Opposite page: The West Gate, Clonmel (1932). Originally part of the medieval wall of the town, this gate was rebuilt in its present form in 1831.

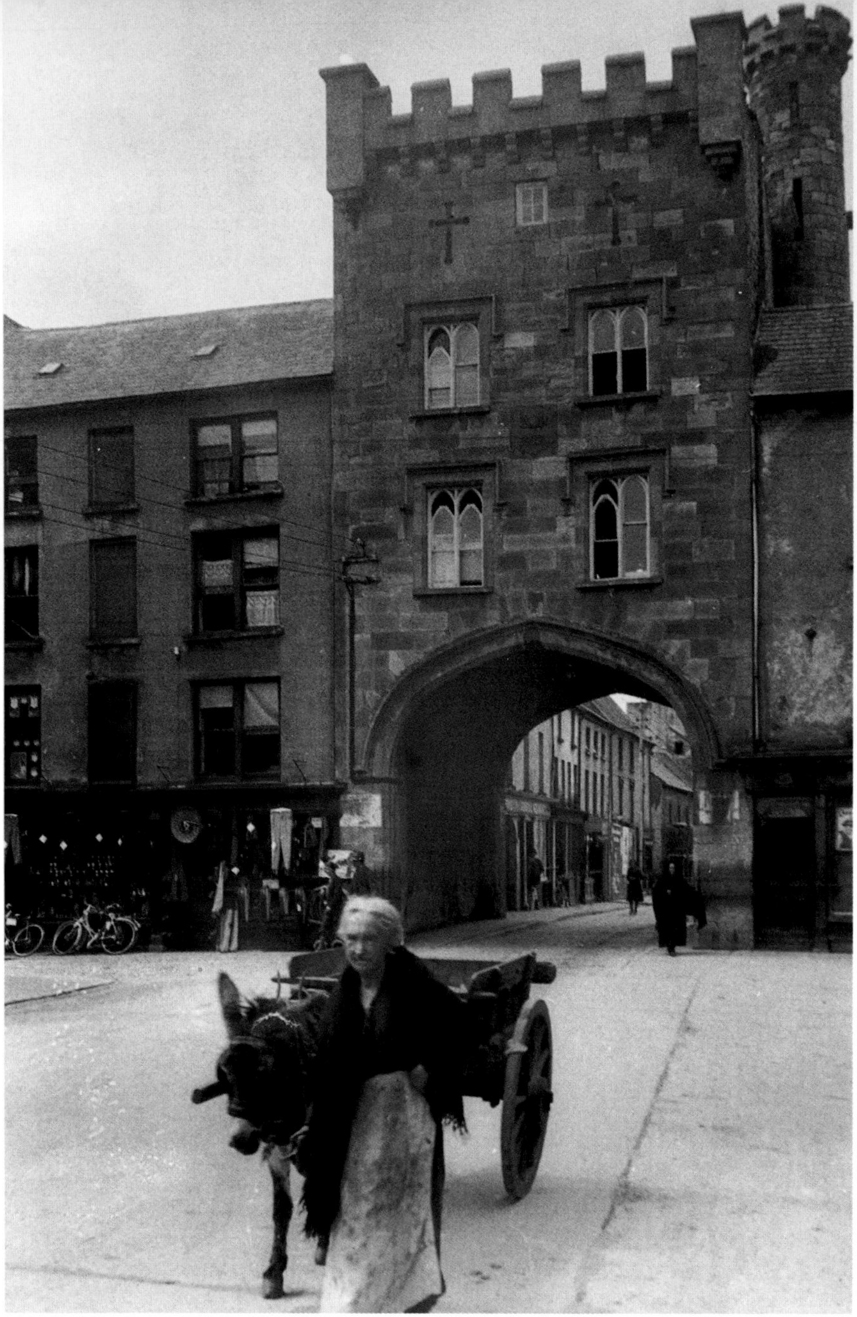

The West Gate, Clonmel (1932), taken from the opposite side. The apron was part of the working woman's attire, whether inside the house or out of doors.

Strolling down from the Round House, Nenagh (1930).

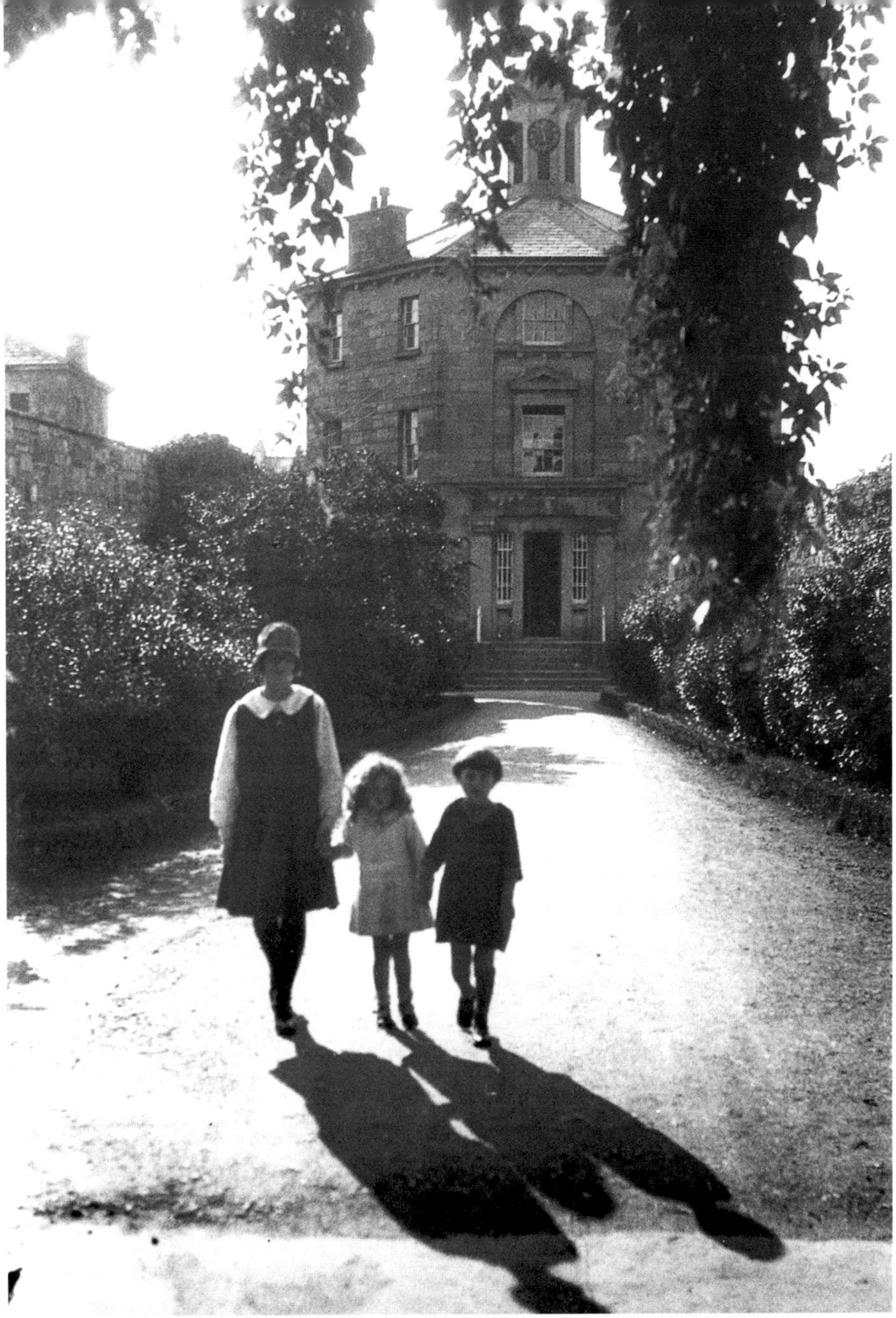

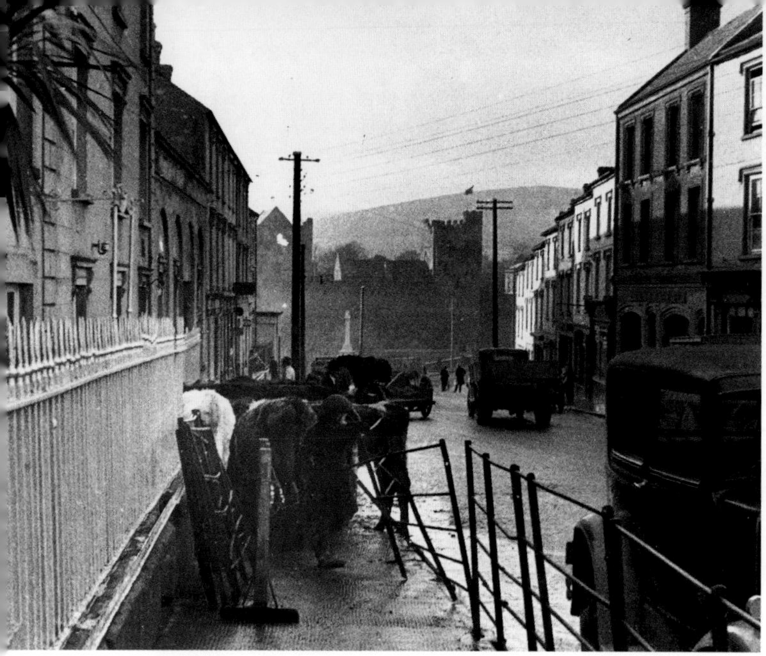

Left: Congestion on the footpath, Cahir (1933). The photograph was taken early on a May morning, as can be seen from the shadows cast by the rising sun.

Below: Mass-goers on their way home from the Church of the Sacred Heart, Templemore (1937).

Opposite page: Street scene, Carrick-on-Suir (1936). This is a noteworthy street scene because it was the last photograph to be taken of these houses that were about to be demolished.

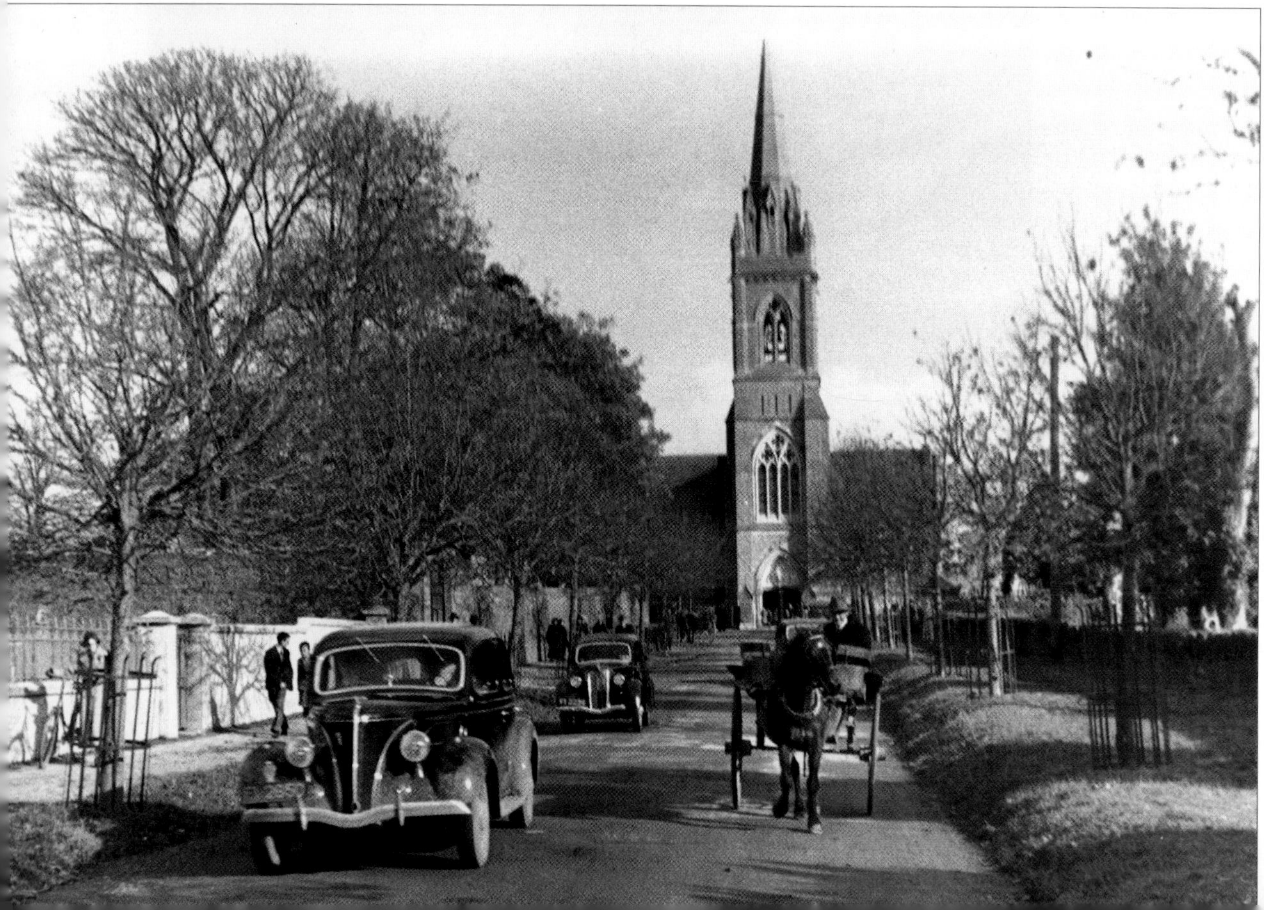

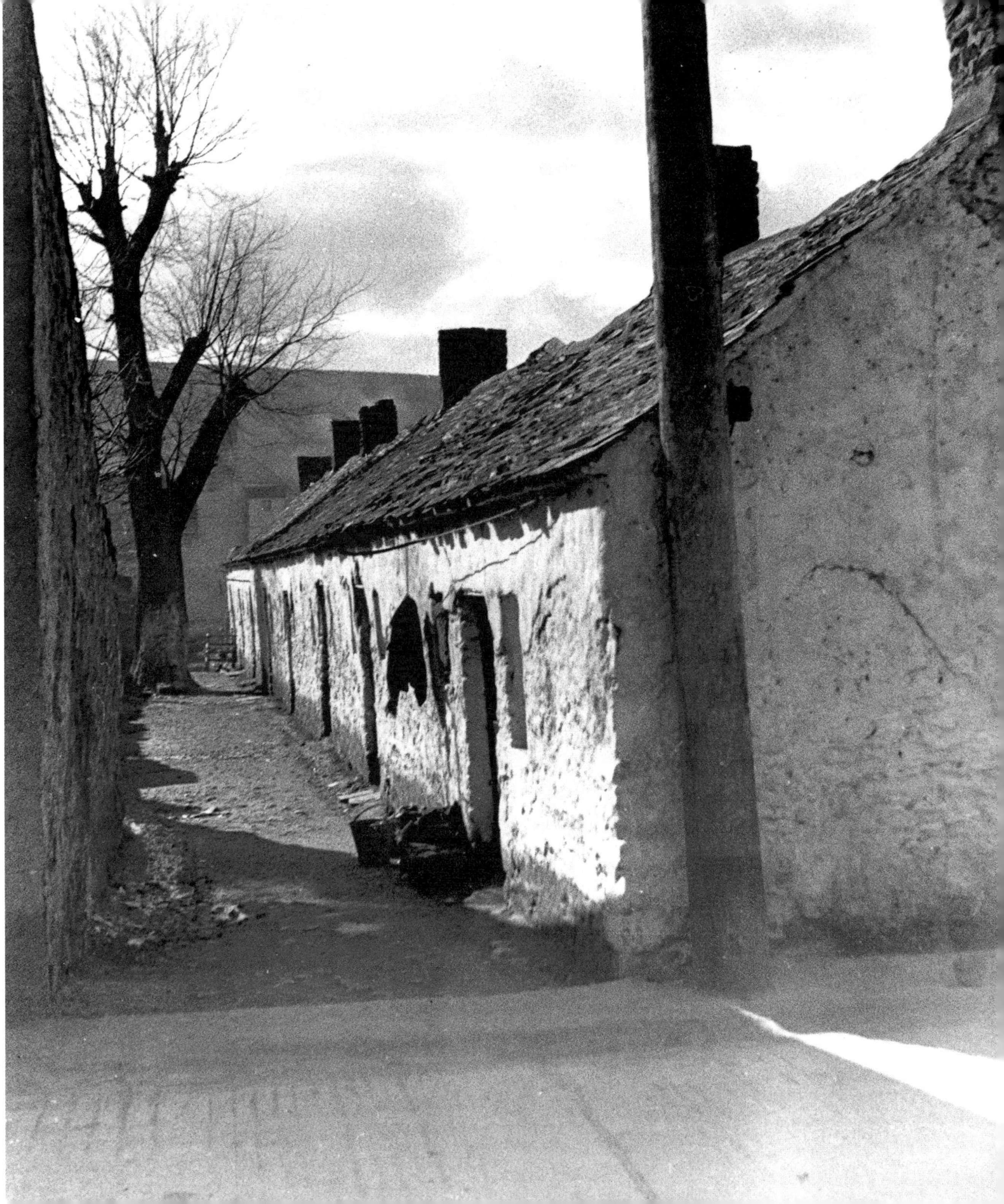

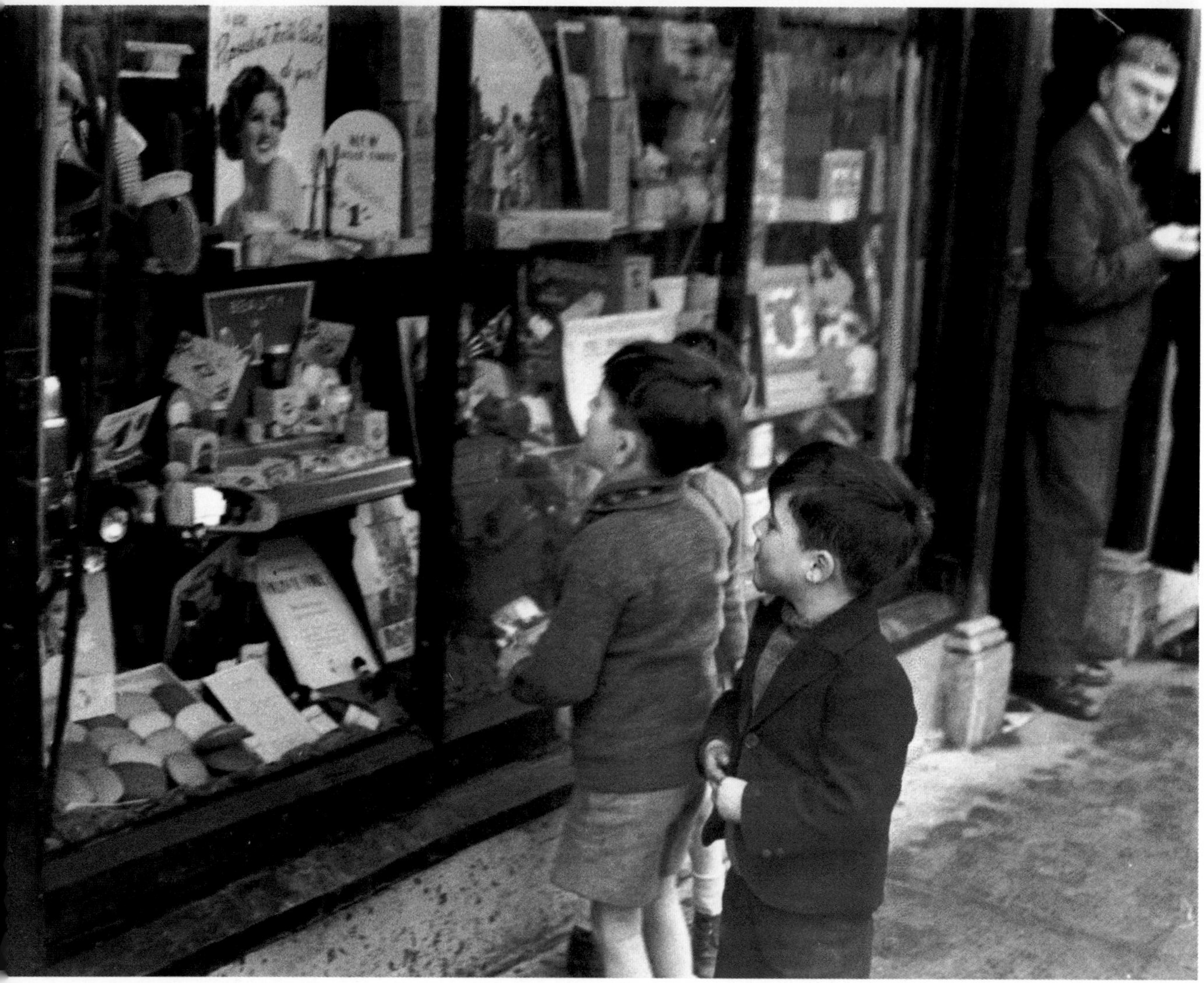

Window-shopping in Templemore (1937).

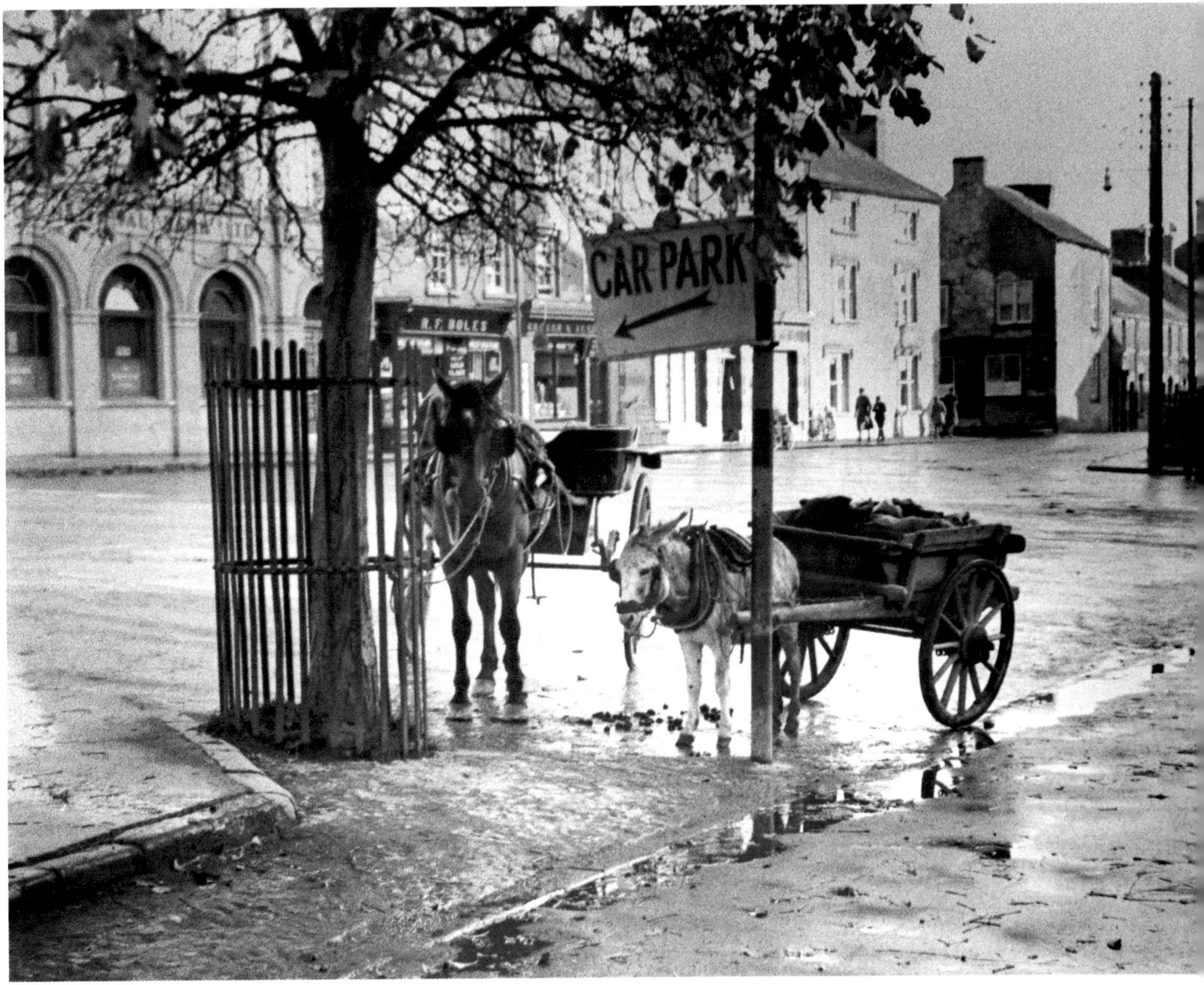

The 'Car Park', Cahir (1942). The scarcity of petrol during the war years explains the absence of cars.

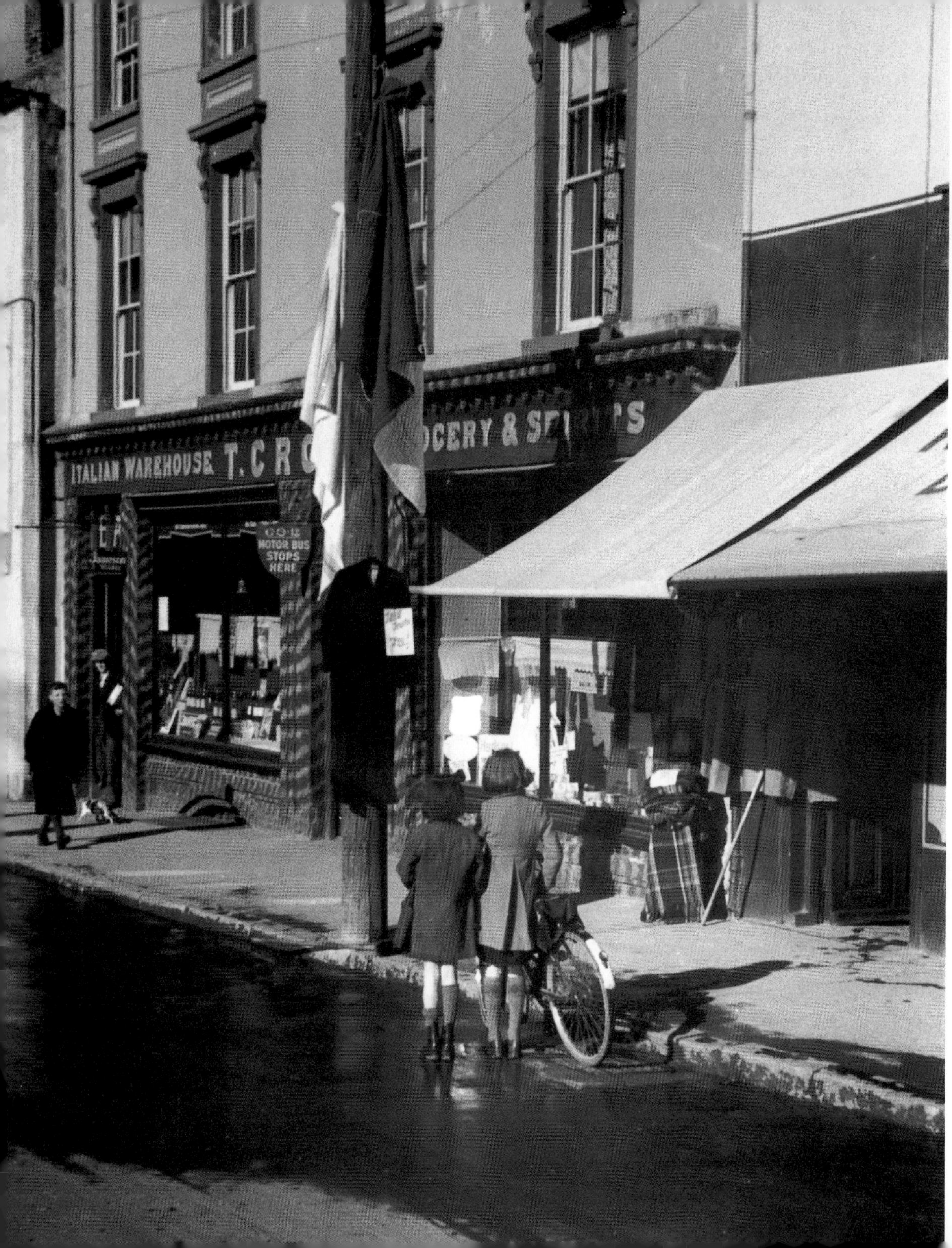
ITALIAN WAREHOUSE
MOTOR BUS
STOPS
HERE

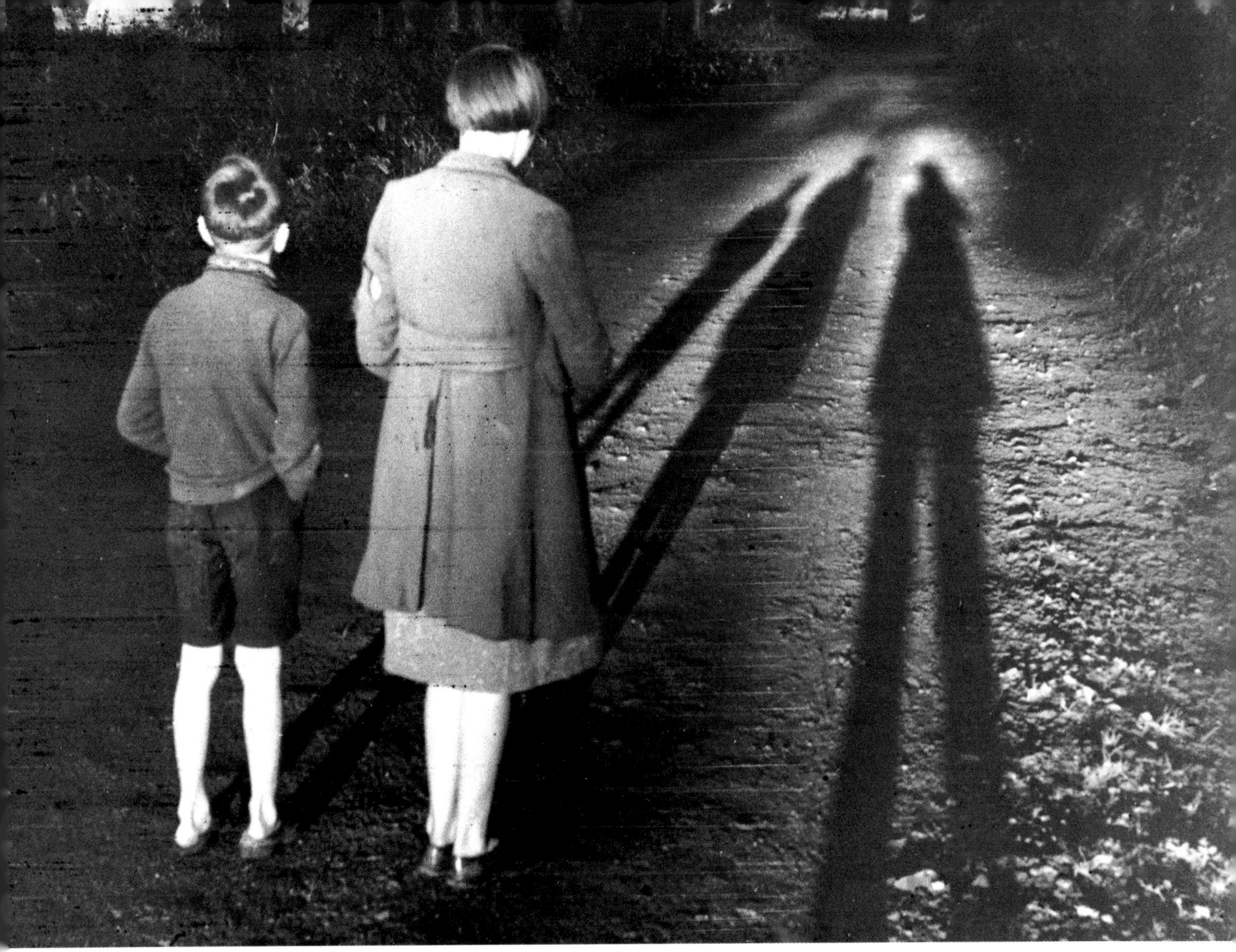

Spooky shadows at Fethard (1938): the photographer's is the one on the right.

Opposite page: Outside the premises of T. Croke, grocer and spirits merchant, Cahir (1942).

Castles

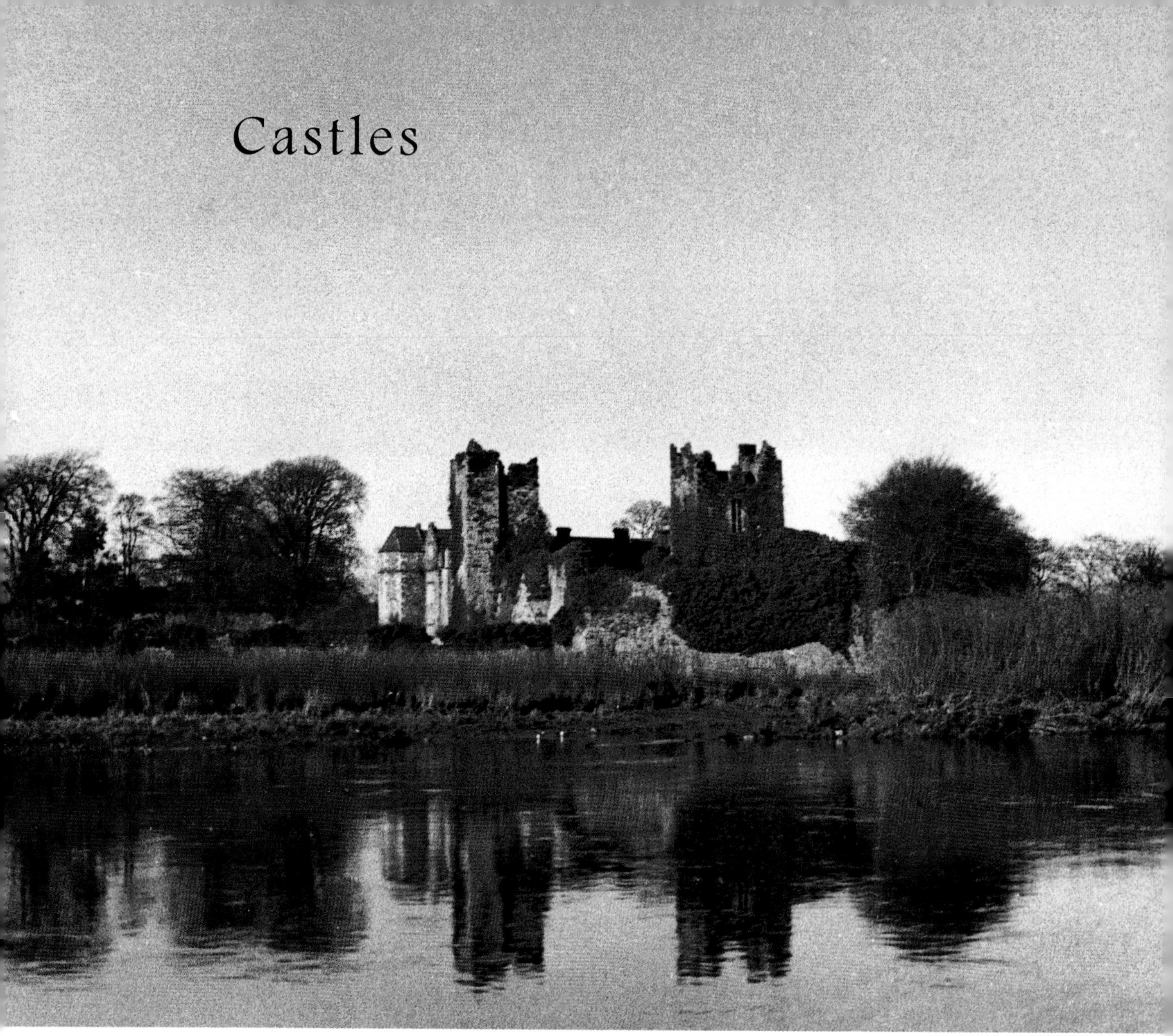

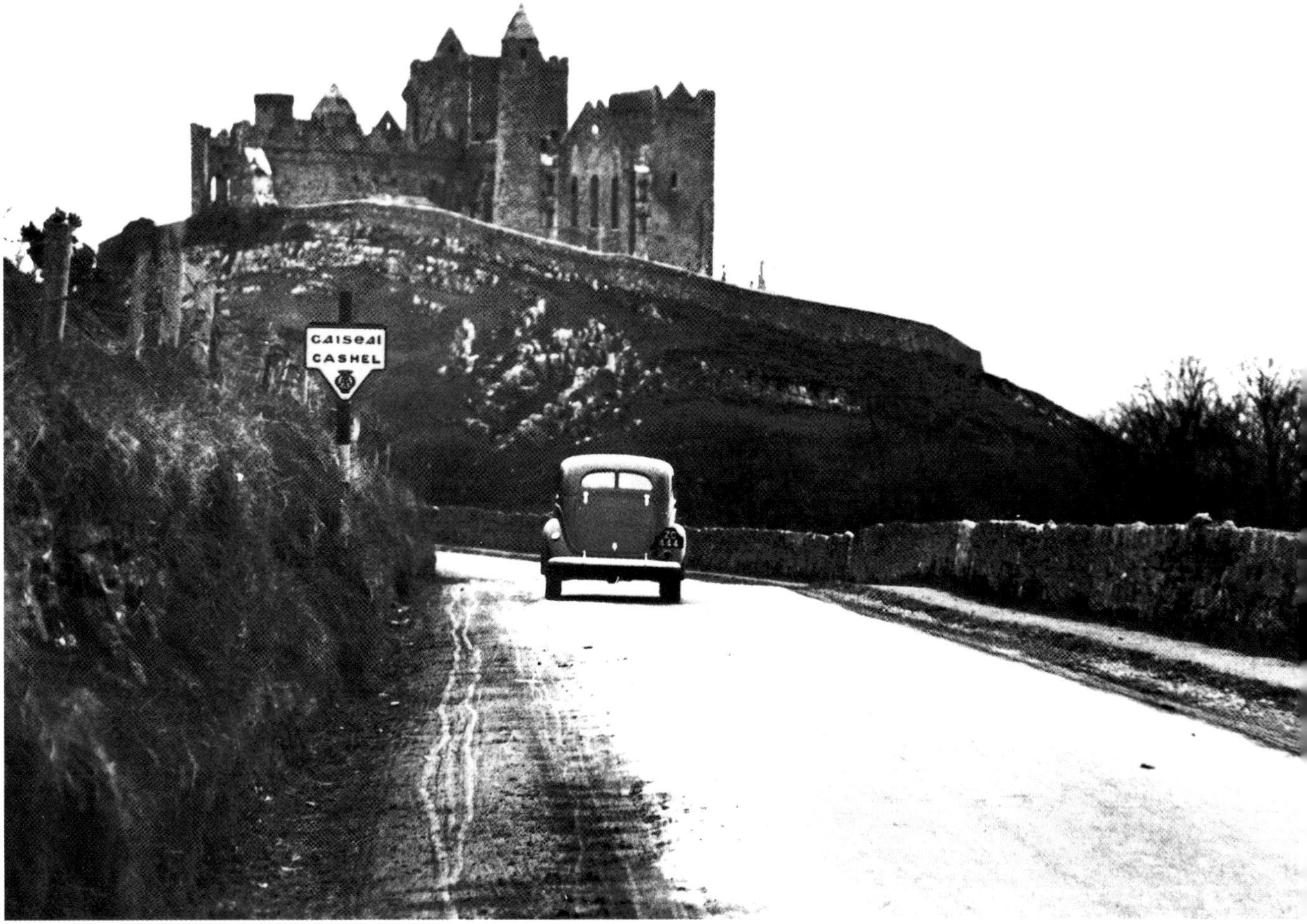

The Rock of Cashel (1939), ancient royal and religious centre of Munster, remains an imposing and unforgettable sight when approached from the Dublin road.

Opposite page: The Ormond Castle at Carrick-on-Suir, taken from the south side of the river (1933). Built in 1450, it was enlarged in 1568 and is said to be the best example of Elizabethan architecture in Ireland.

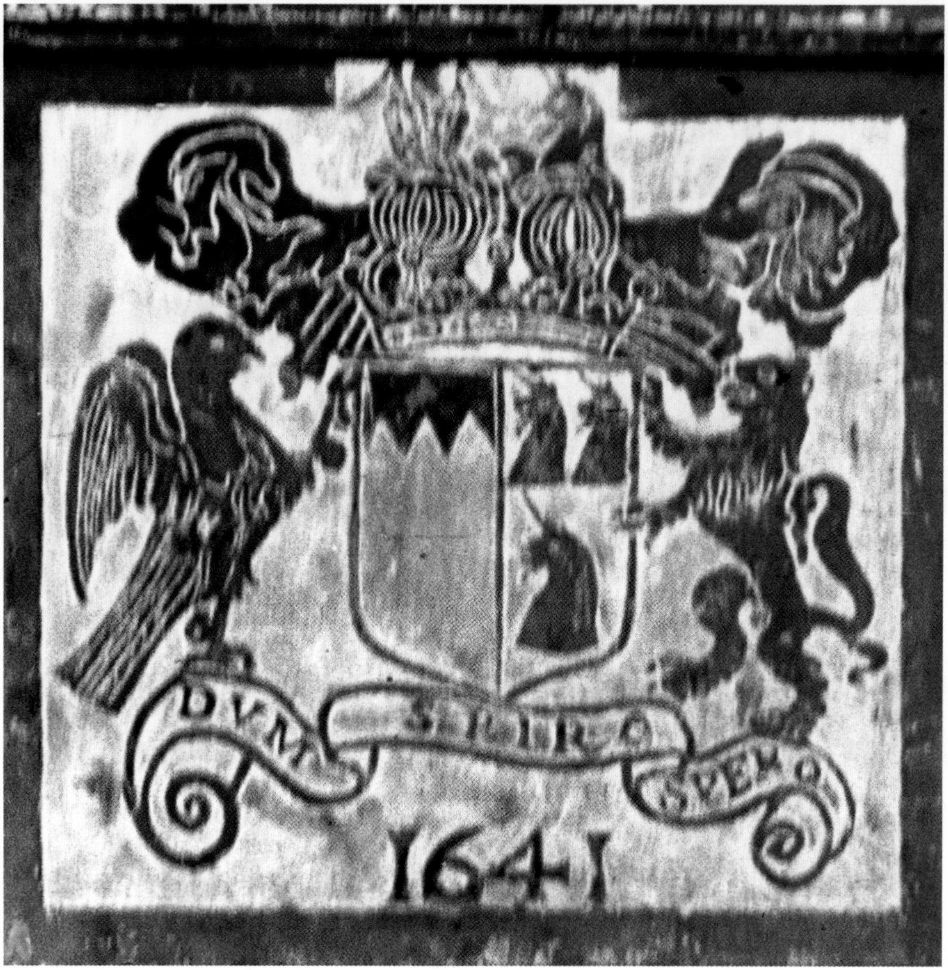

Carrick Castle (1944). The family crest on the Eastern Saloon wall, clearly dated 1641, bears the motto 'Dum Spiro Spero', i.e. 'So long as I breathe, I keep hope.'

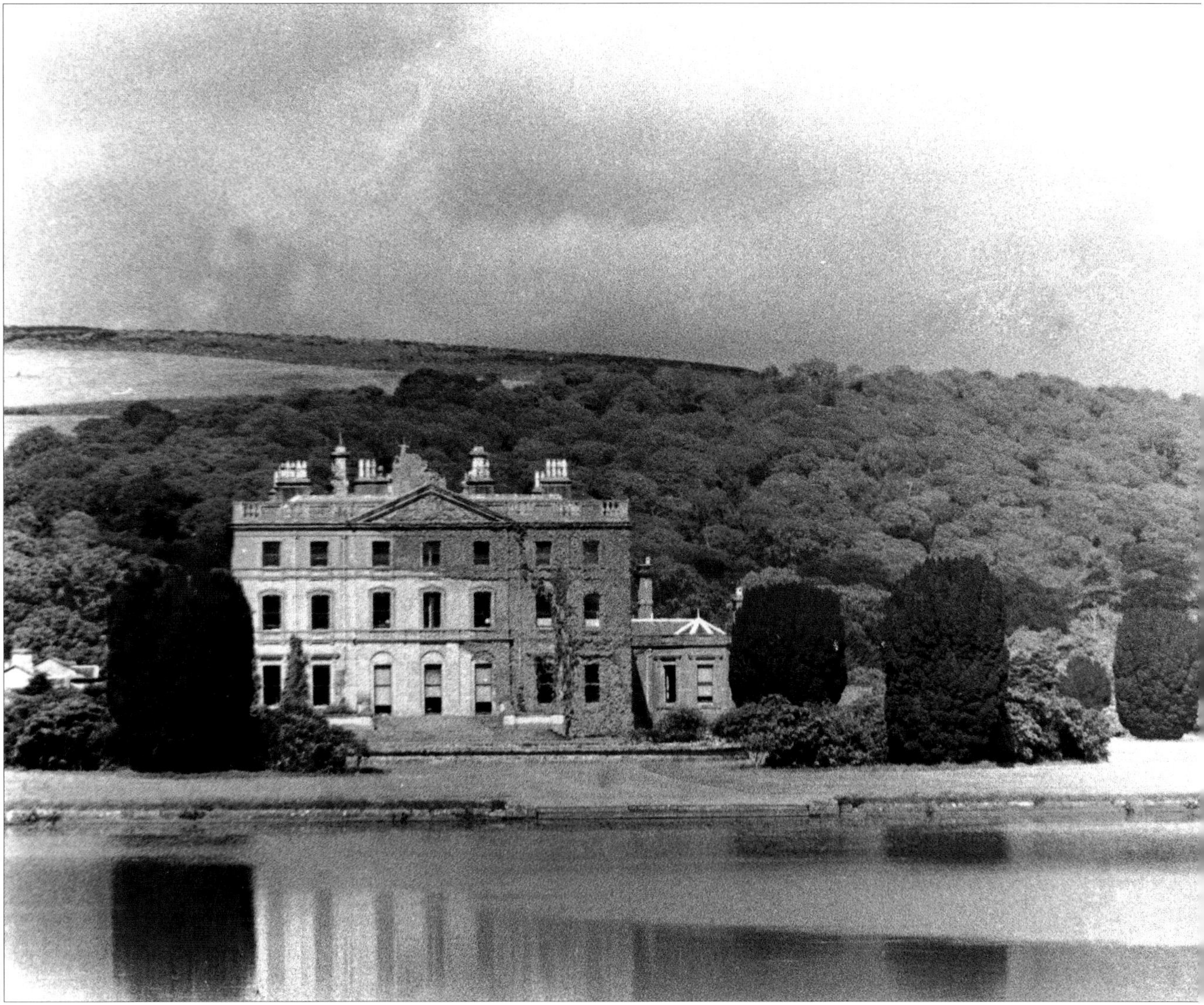

Carrick Castle, looking across the River Suir (1944).

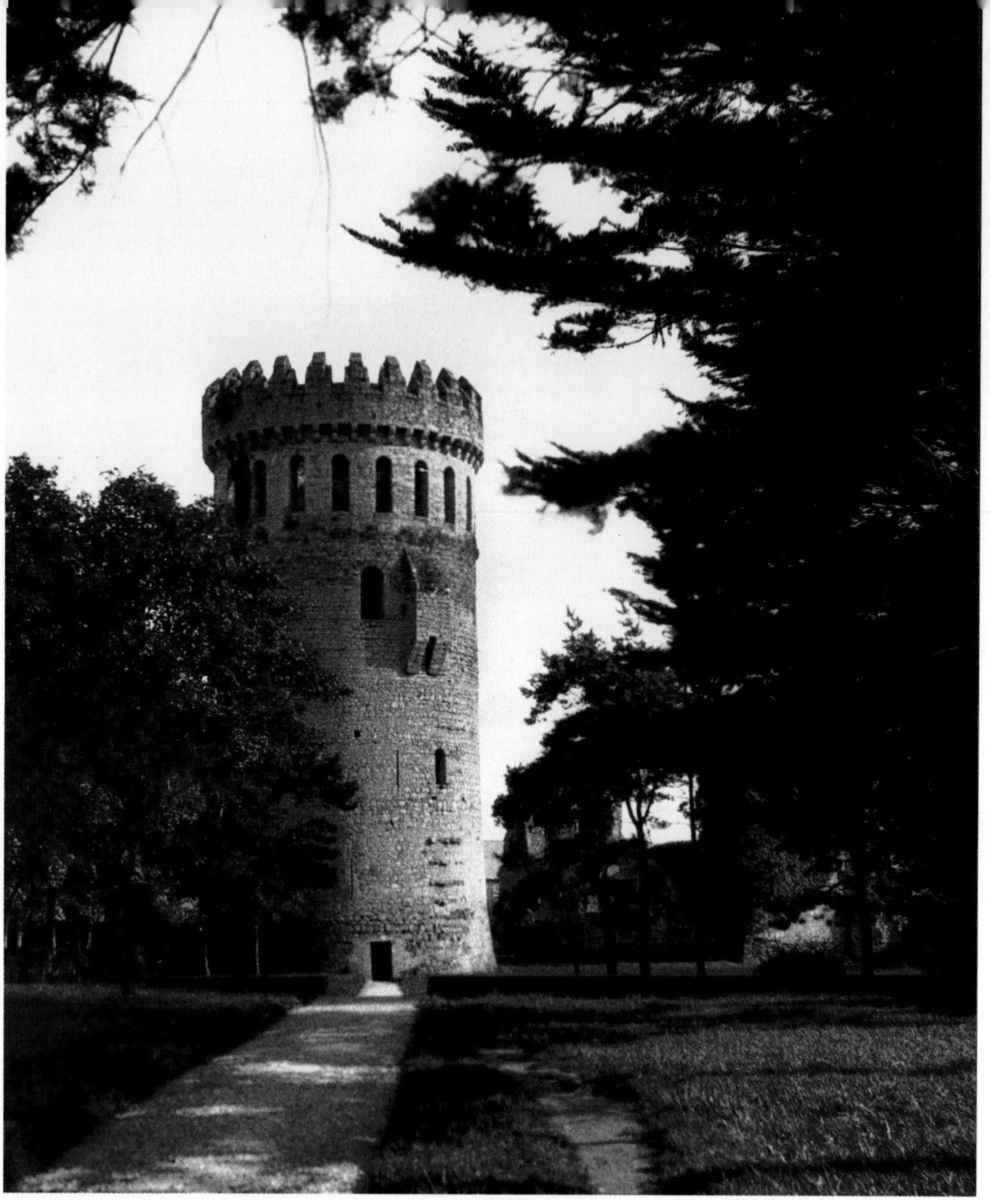

Nenagh Castle (1930). This imposing tower was one of the three donjons along the curtain wall of the Norman castle which was built here by Theobald Walter, nephew of Thomas à Becket, at the start of the thirteenth century.

The Ormonde Castle, Main Street, Roscrea (1930). Built in the thirteenth century, the gable and chimney seen here were added in the seventeenth century.

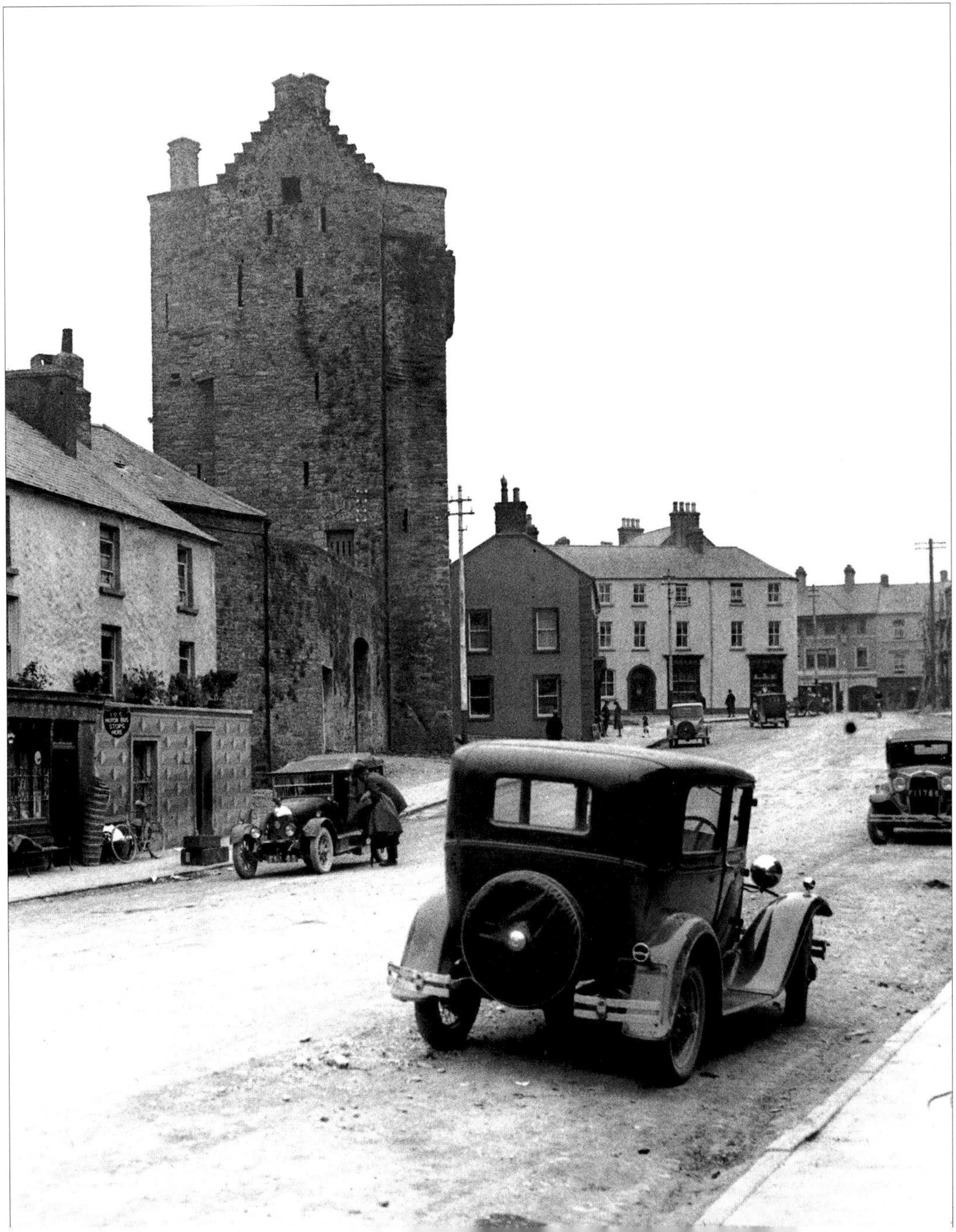

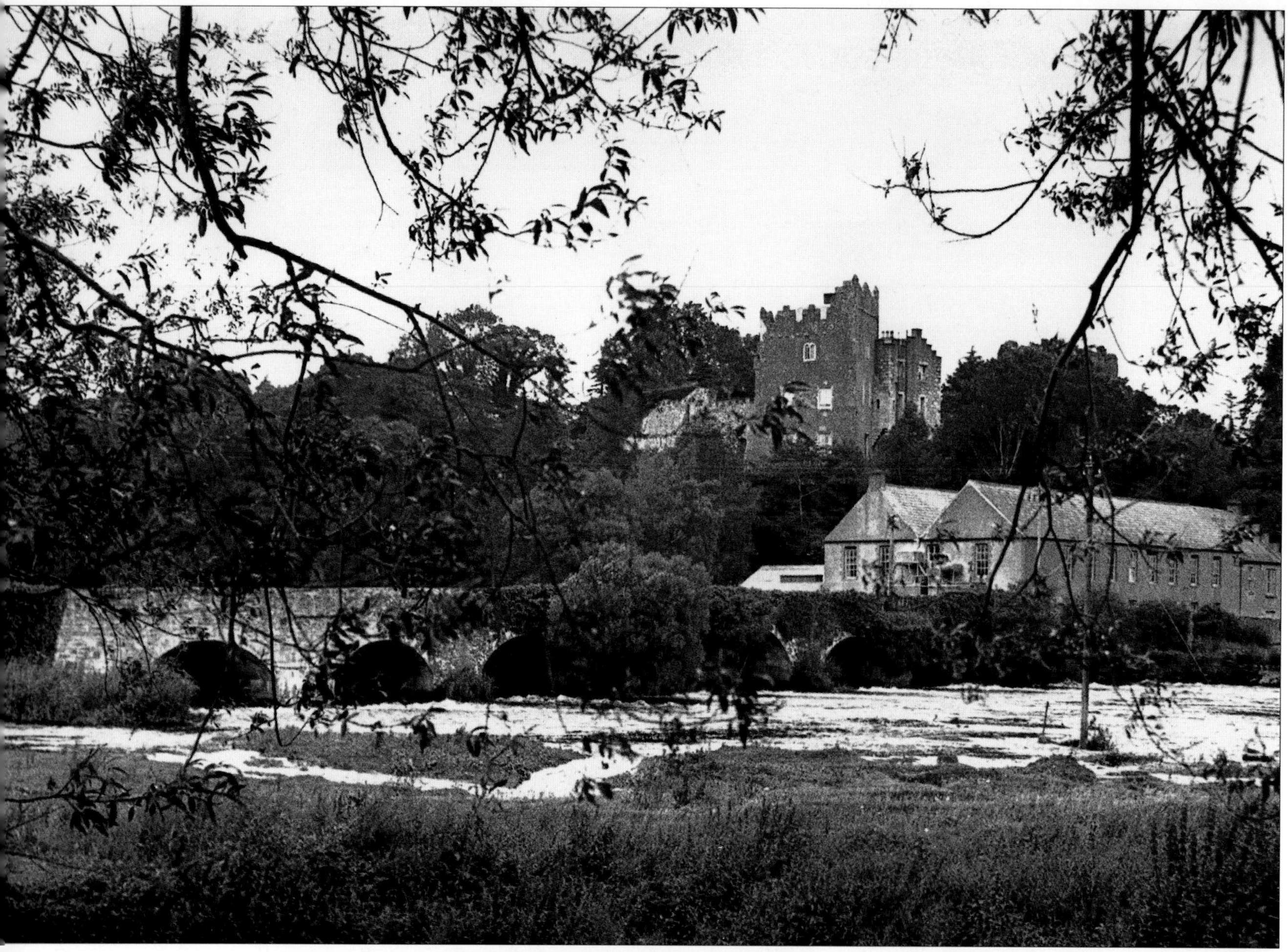

Ardfinnane Castle stands above the River Suir about halfway between Clonmel and Cahir (1931).

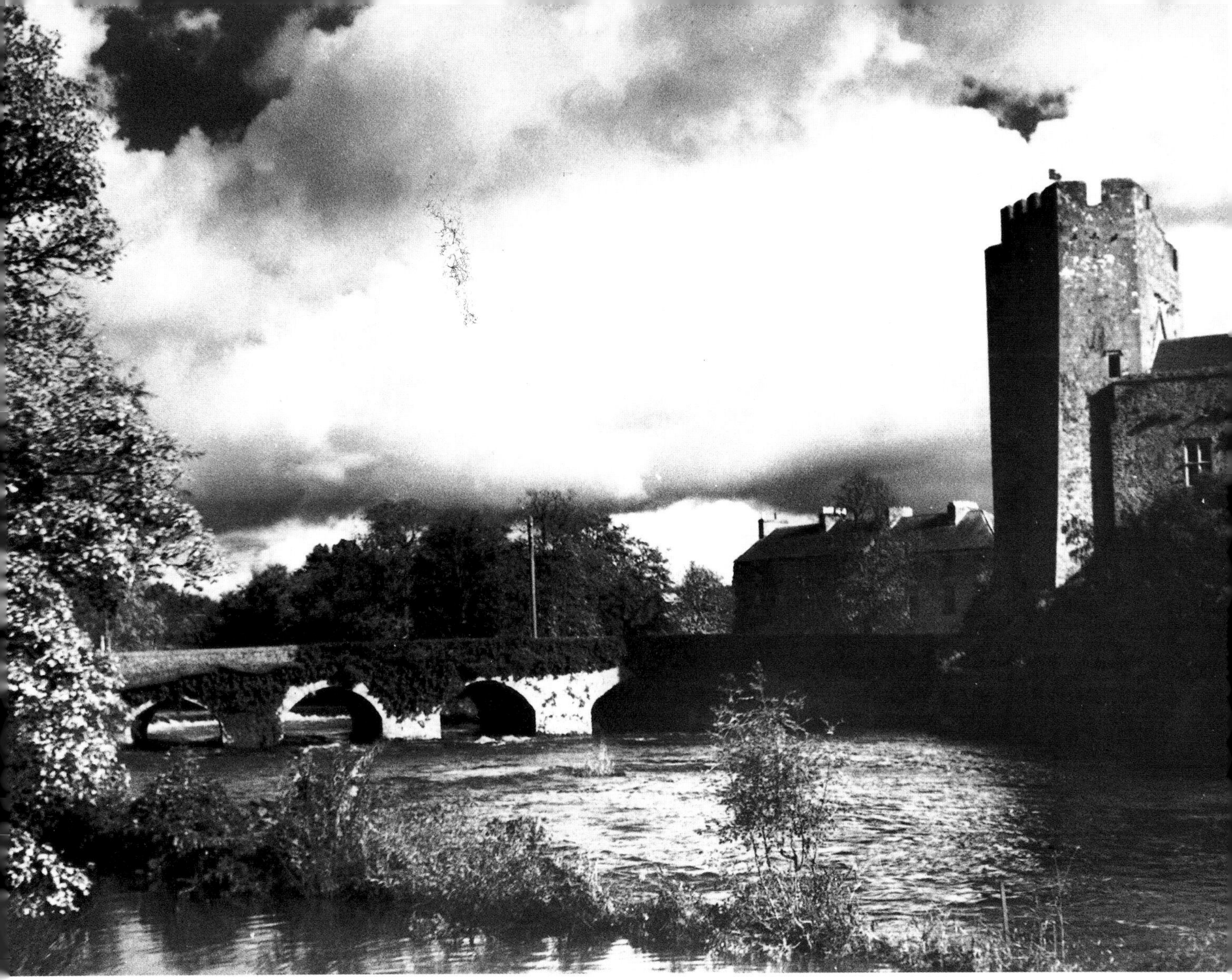

Cahir Castle (1942). The original castle here was built by the O'Briens of Thomond in 1169. This one was built by James Butler, Earl of Ormond, towards the end of the fourteenth century. The castle has been renovated and is now open to the public.

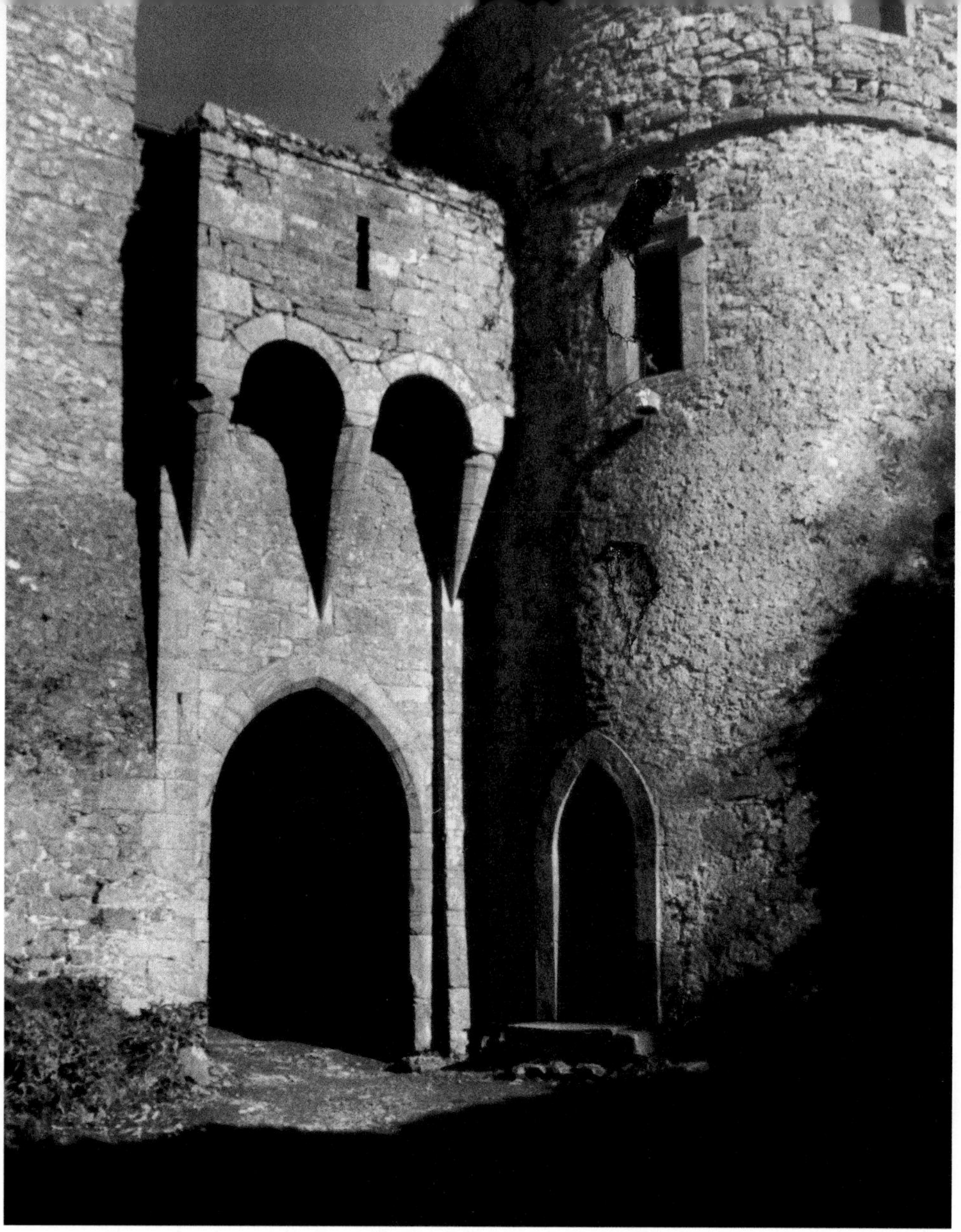

Cahir Castle (1942). The first of two gates between the middle and inner wards showing the flanking tower and the machicoulis down which unspeakable objects could be dropped on the unwary intruder.

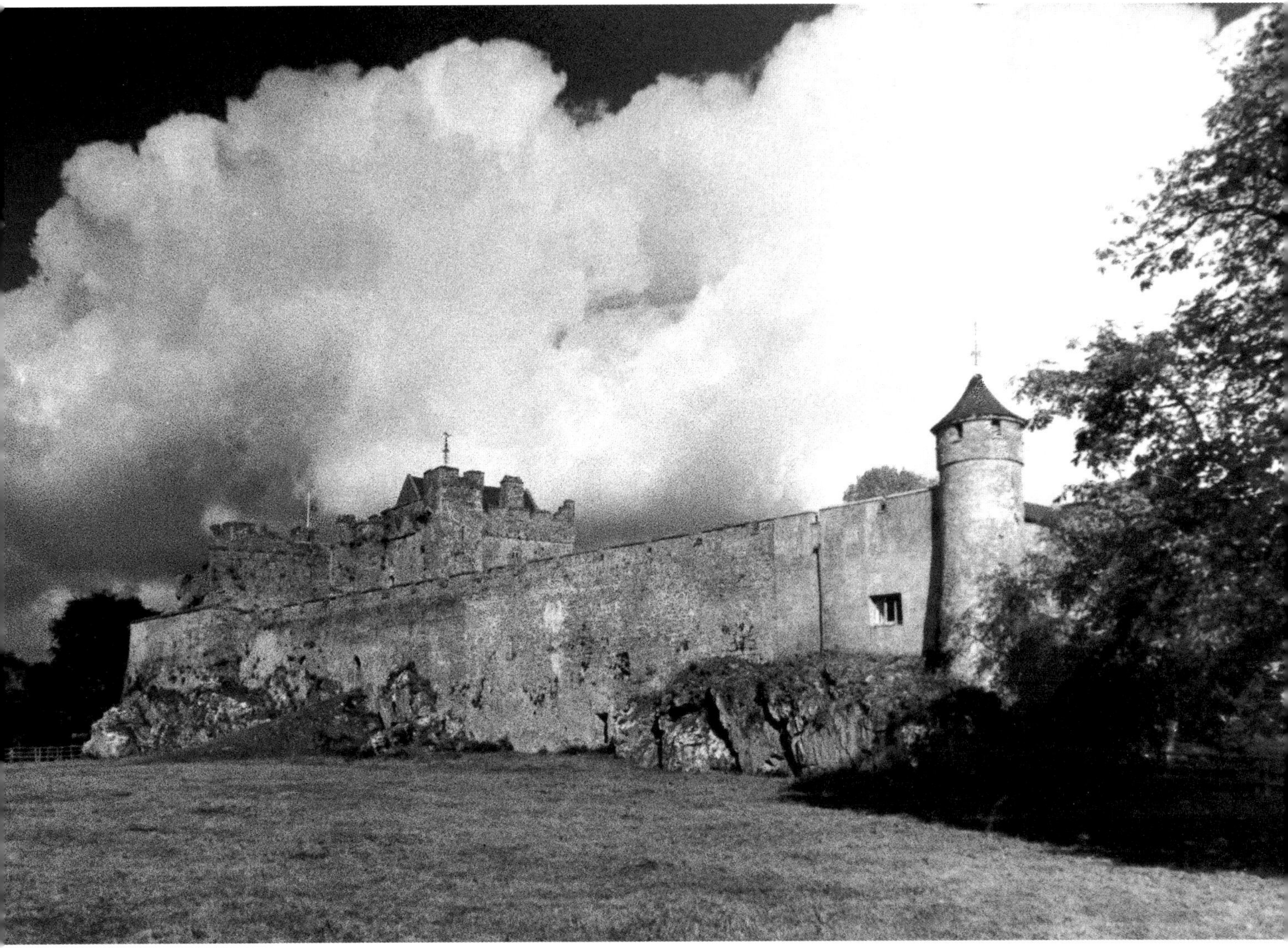

Cahir Castle (1942). Dating from the end of the fourteenth century, the outer walls shown here are defended by eight towers, three rectangular and five round.

School and Sport

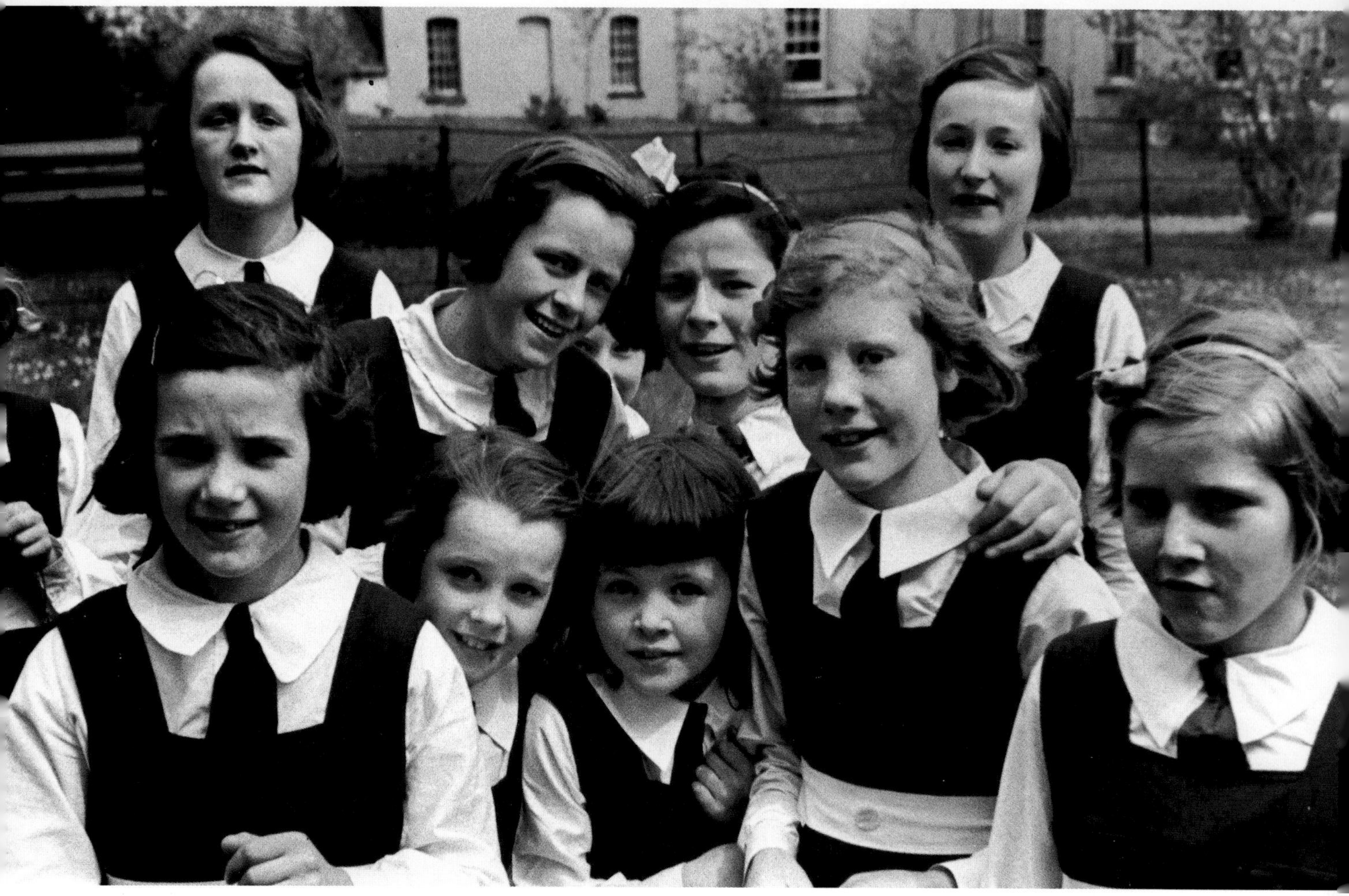

A happy group of girls at St Michael's Orphanage, Dundrum (1944). The Presentation Sisters ran the orphanage here from 1908 to 1975.

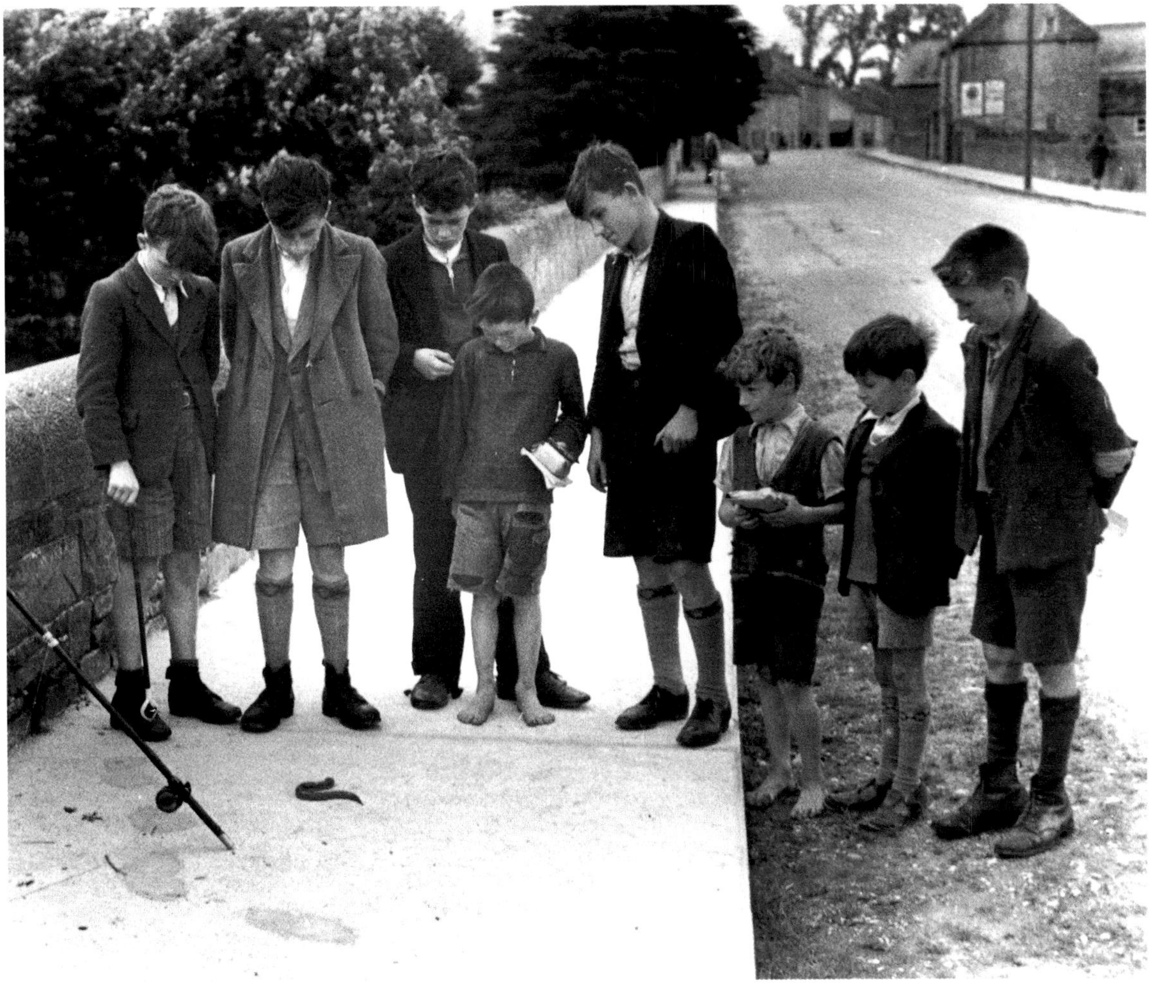

'Some Catch!' (1944). Young anglers admire an eel just taken from the River Suir at Cahir.

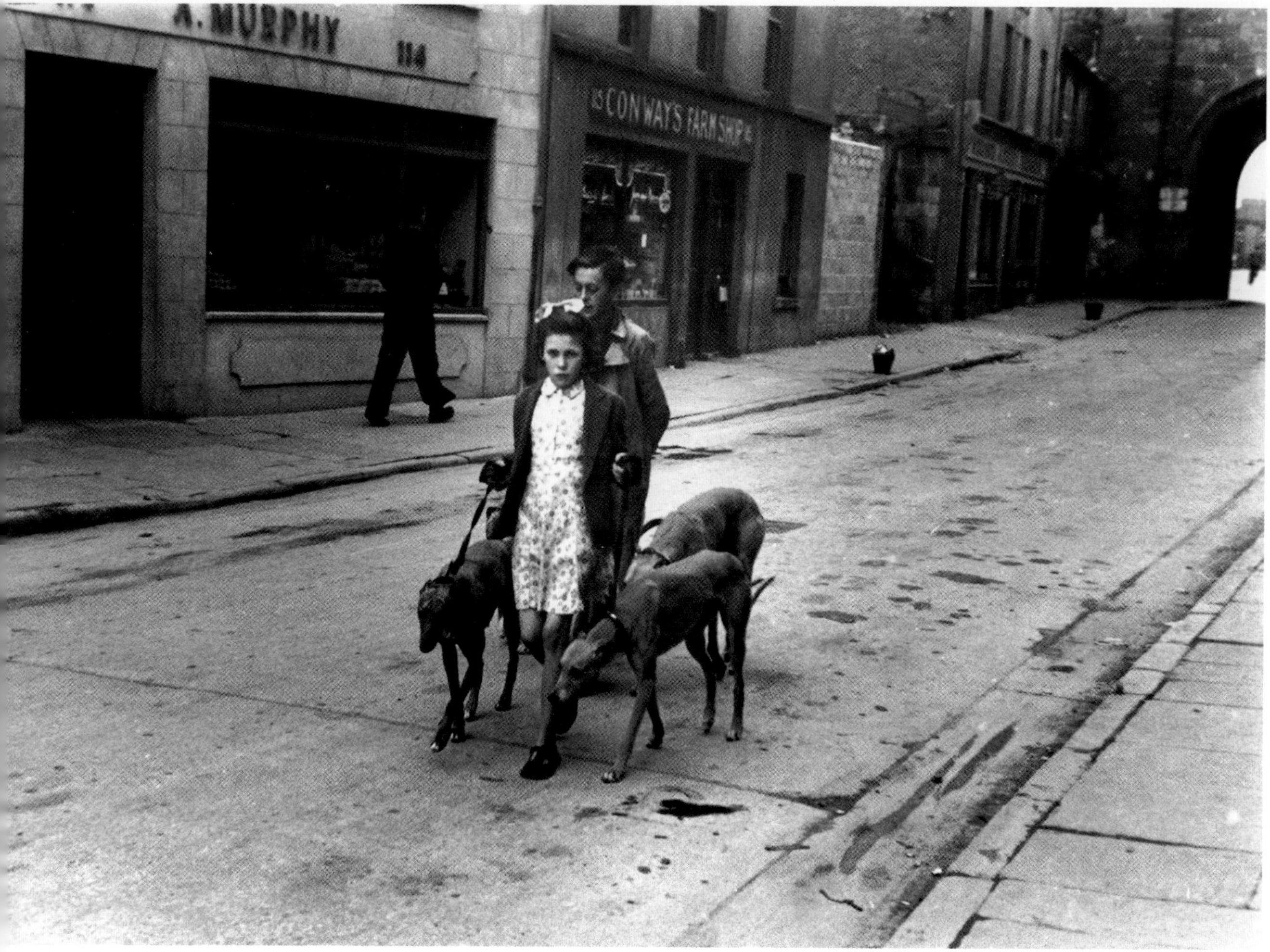

'Walking the Dogs', Clonmel (1947).

Opposite page: Playing 'soldiers' at Thurles (1937). The game was like 'conkers' but played with the heads of cereals and grasses rather than chestnuts.

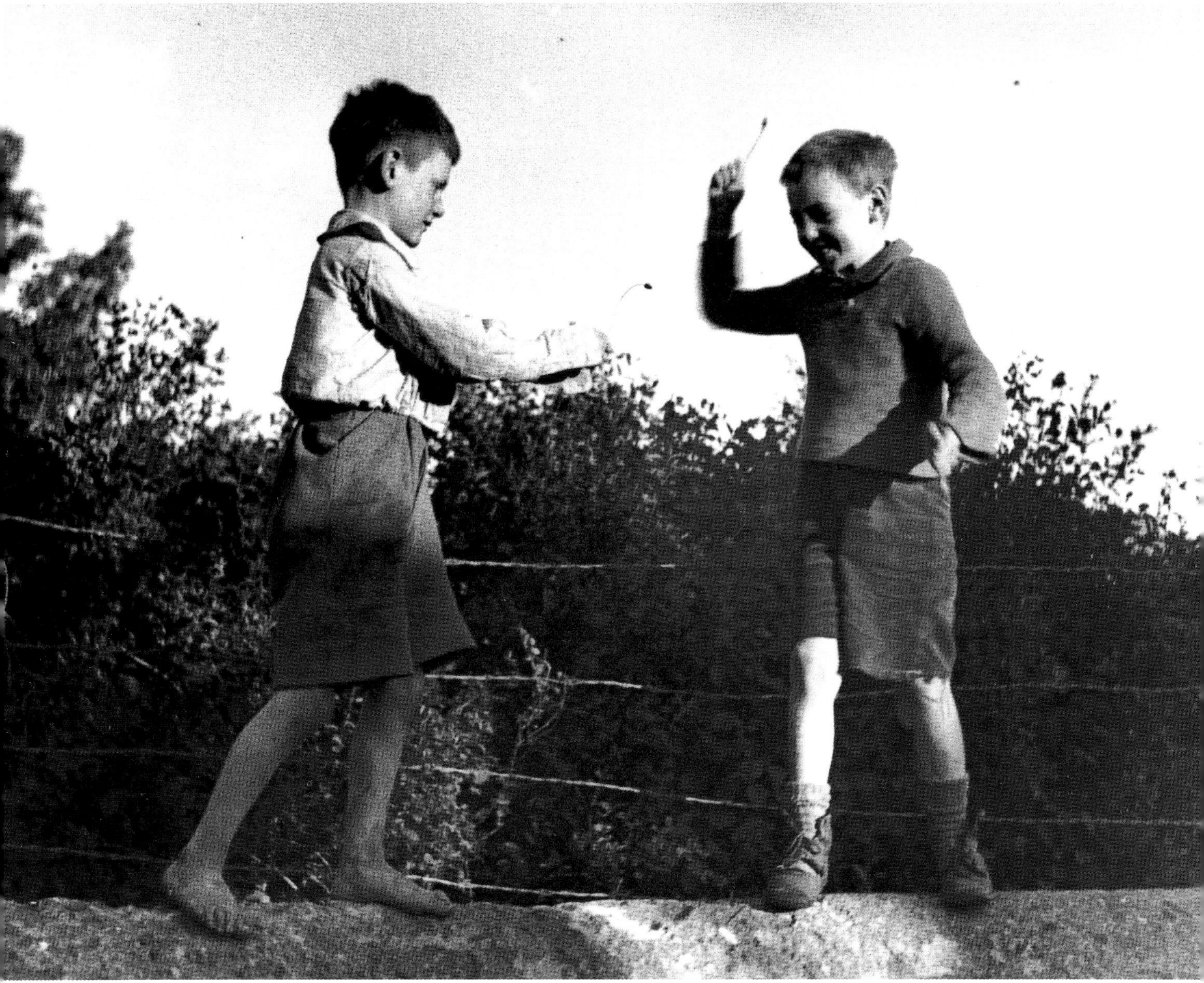

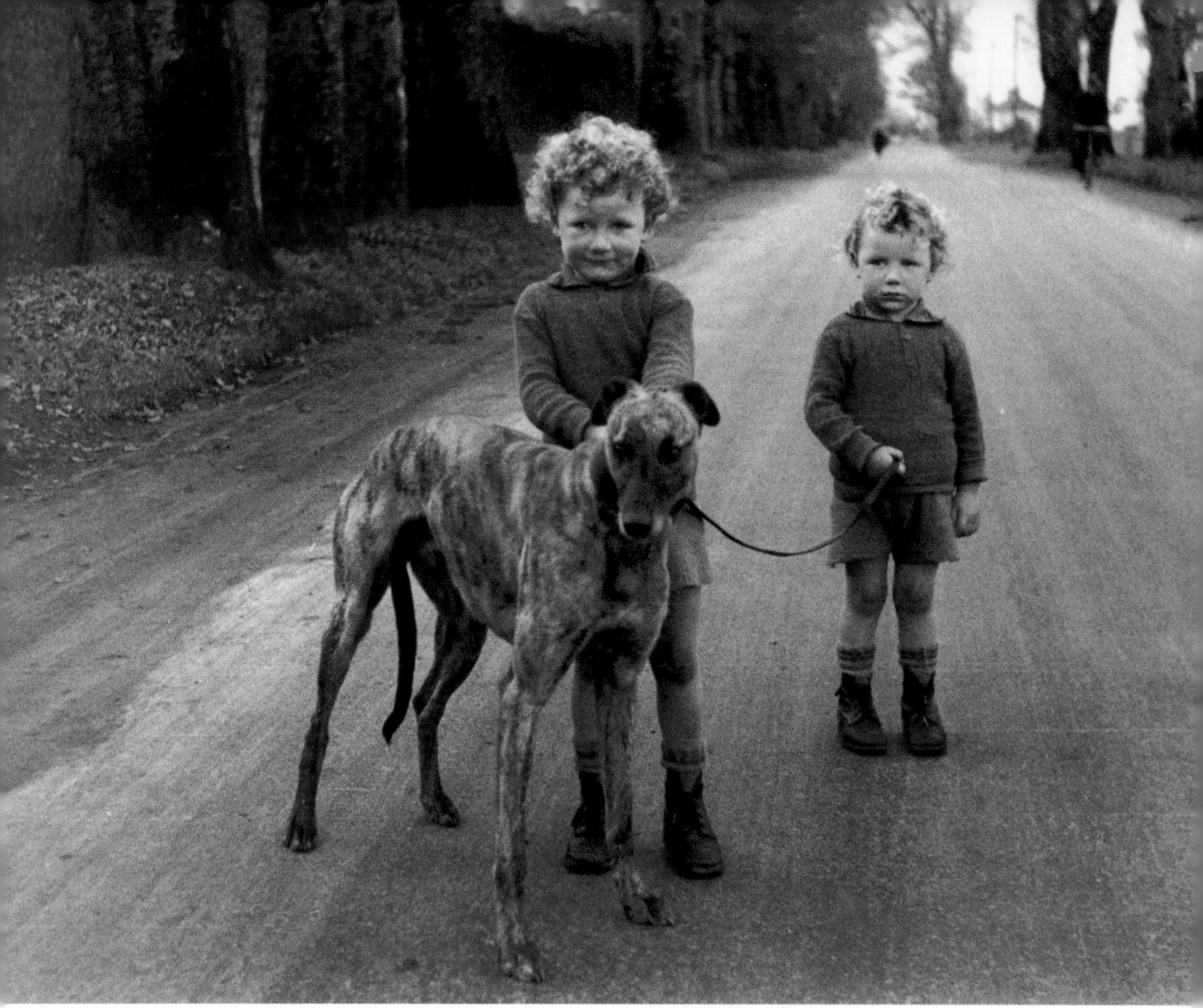

Paddy and Jim Colleran, sons of the local Garda Superintendent, exercise the greyhound at Templemore (1937).

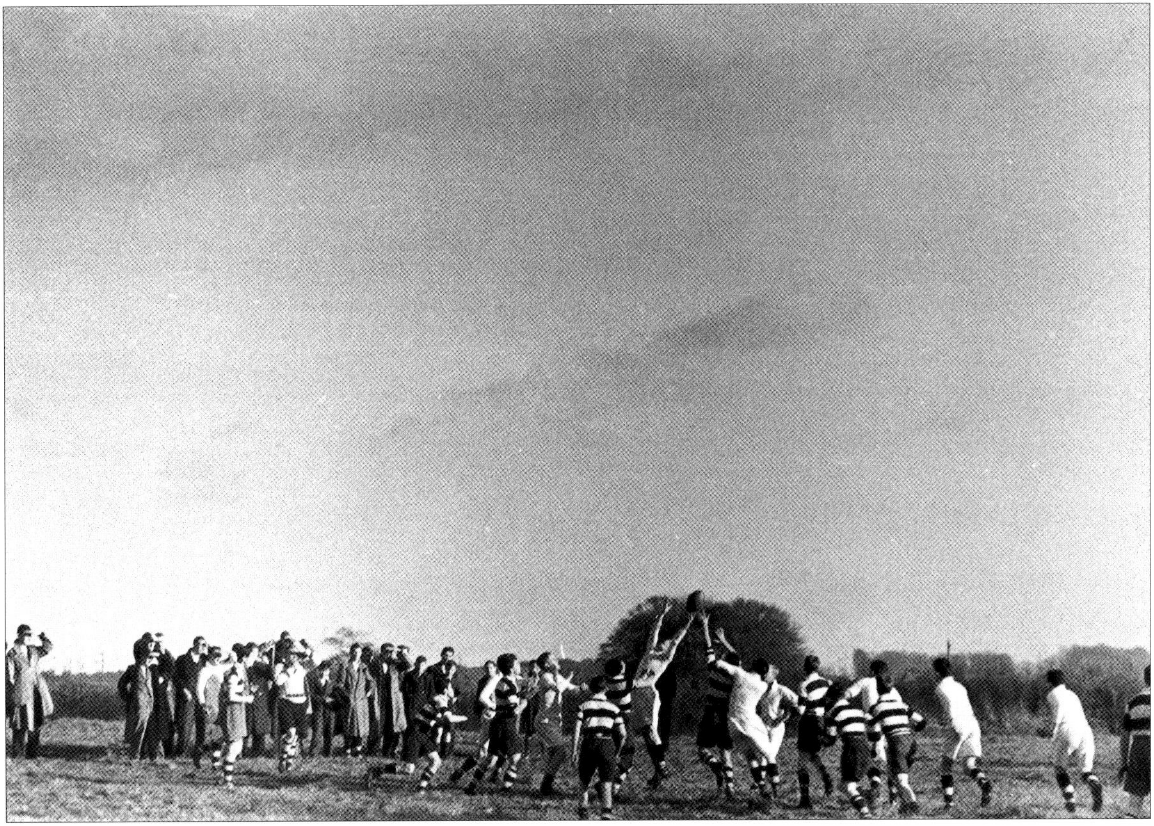

Rugby at Rockwell College, near Cashel (1937). The boys were playing a friendly match with Templemore R.F.C., founded in 1930.

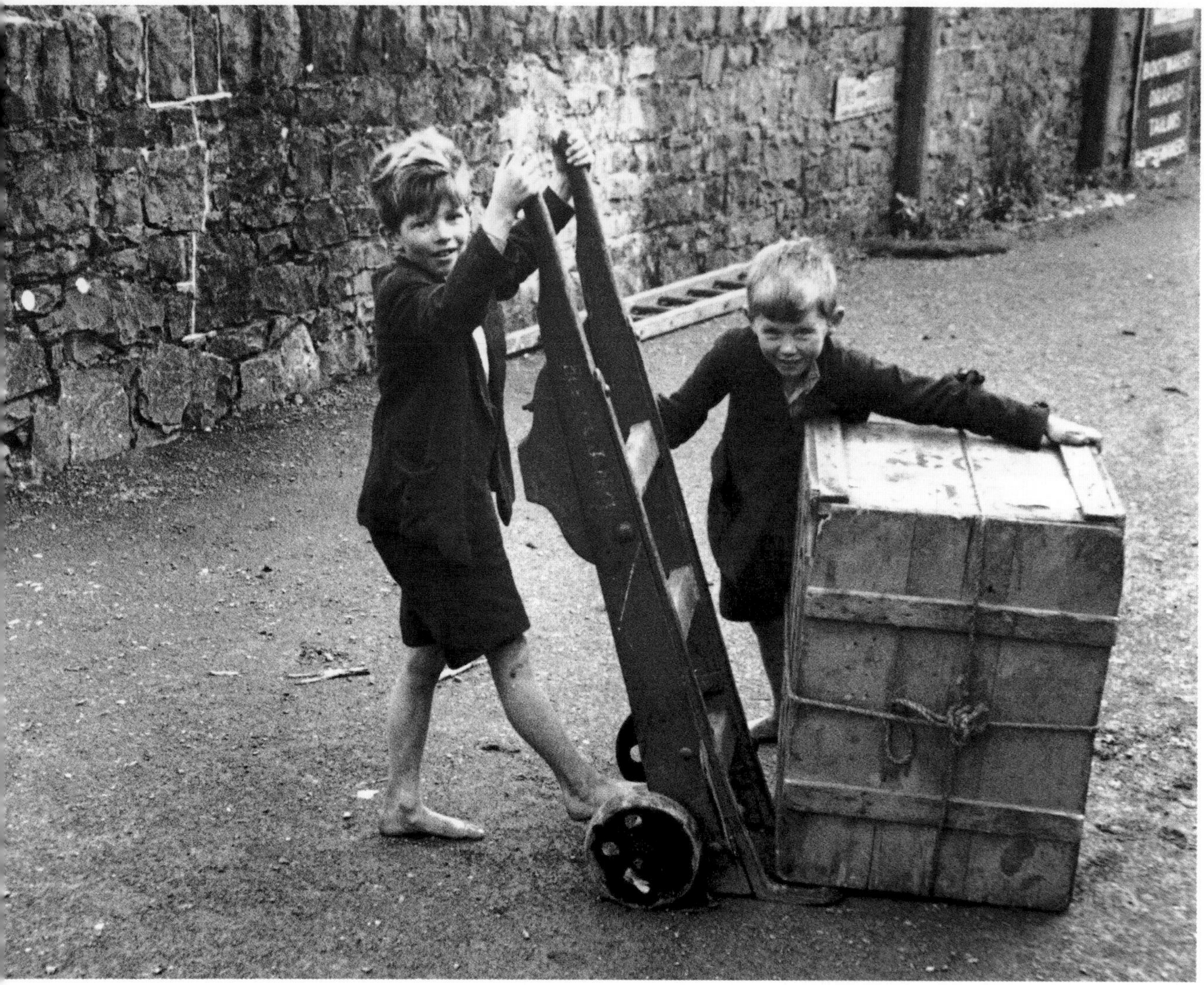

Boys playing porter on the platform of Fethard Railway Station (1938). The railway closed for passengers in 1962. Tony Newport of Fethard framed the last ticket sold and now keeps it as a souvenir in his pub.

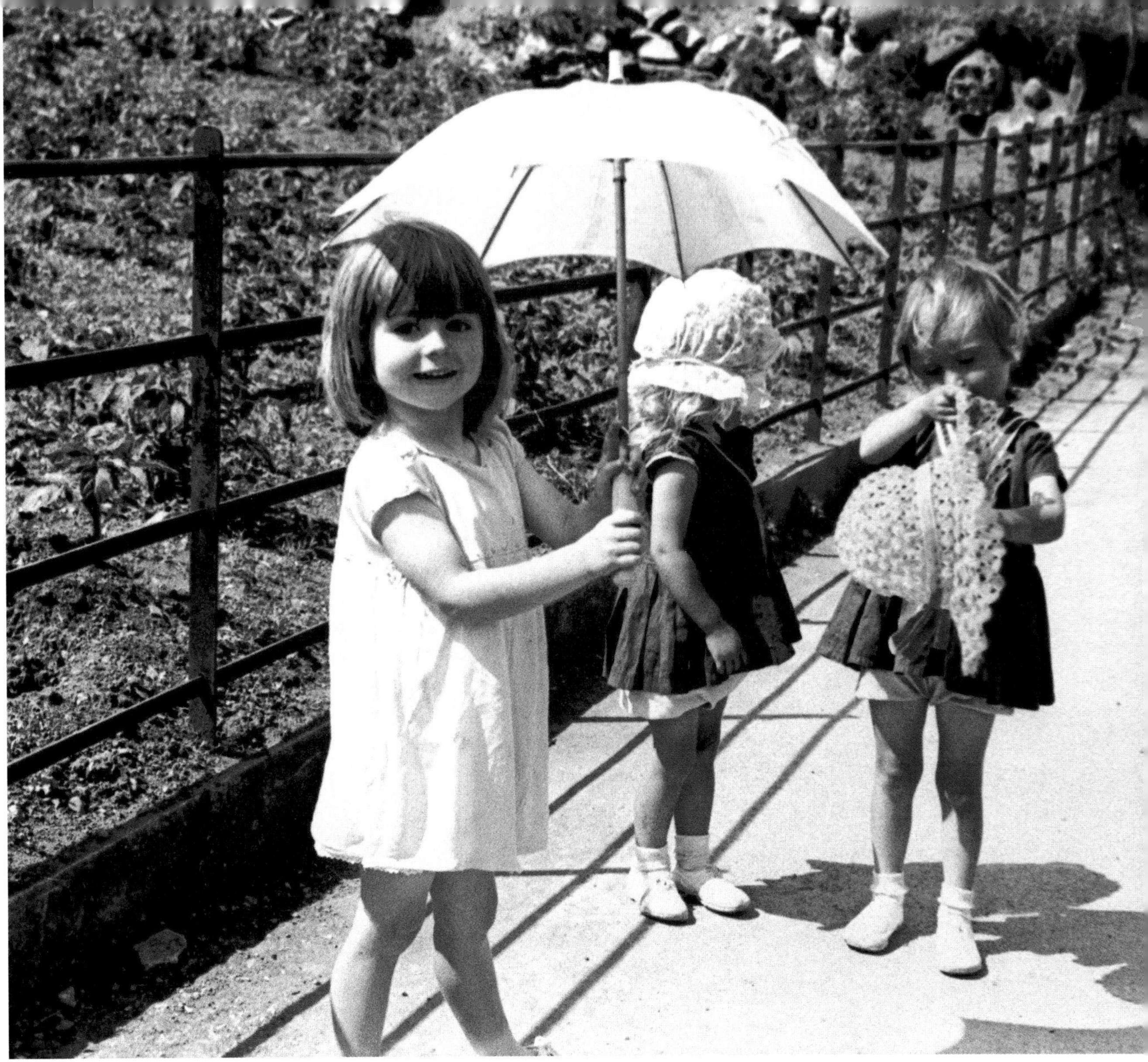

'Parasol Girl', near Tipperary town (1940).

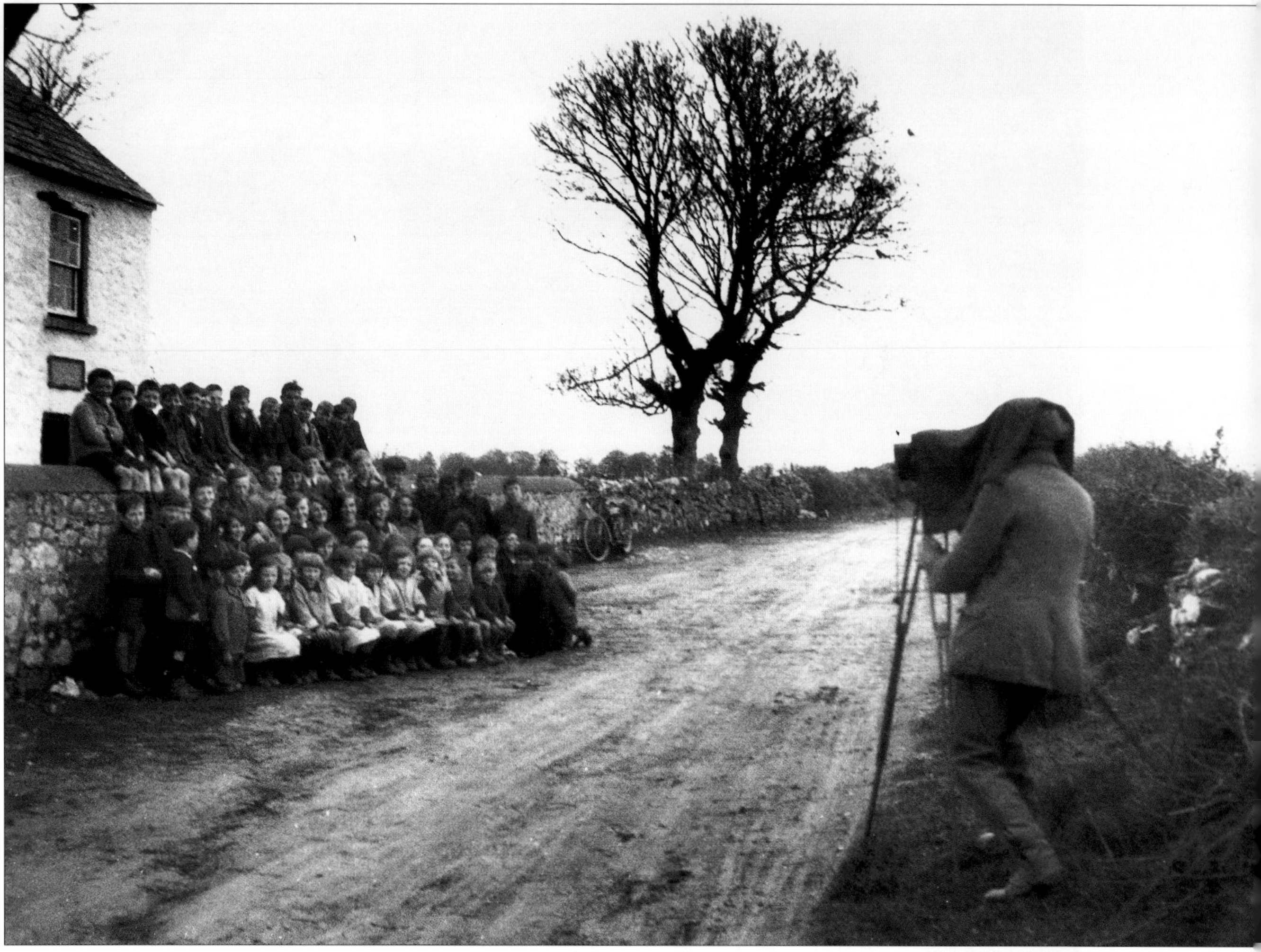

Father Browne photographs the photographer photographing the pupils of Golden National School.

Opposite page: The 'Black and Tans' in full cry (1933), taken near Scarteen where the famous pack of fox-hounds was based.

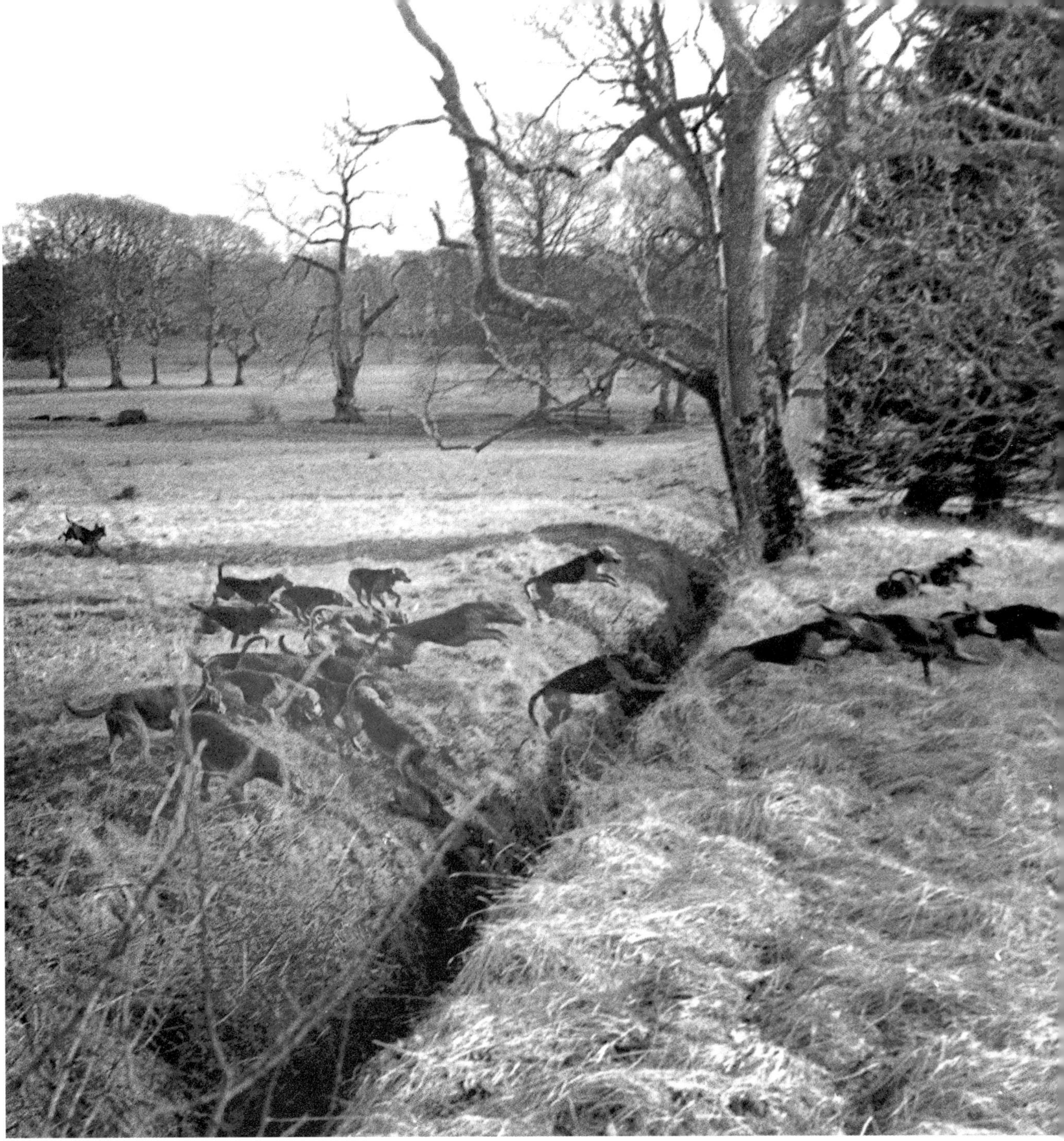

Monasteries and Churches

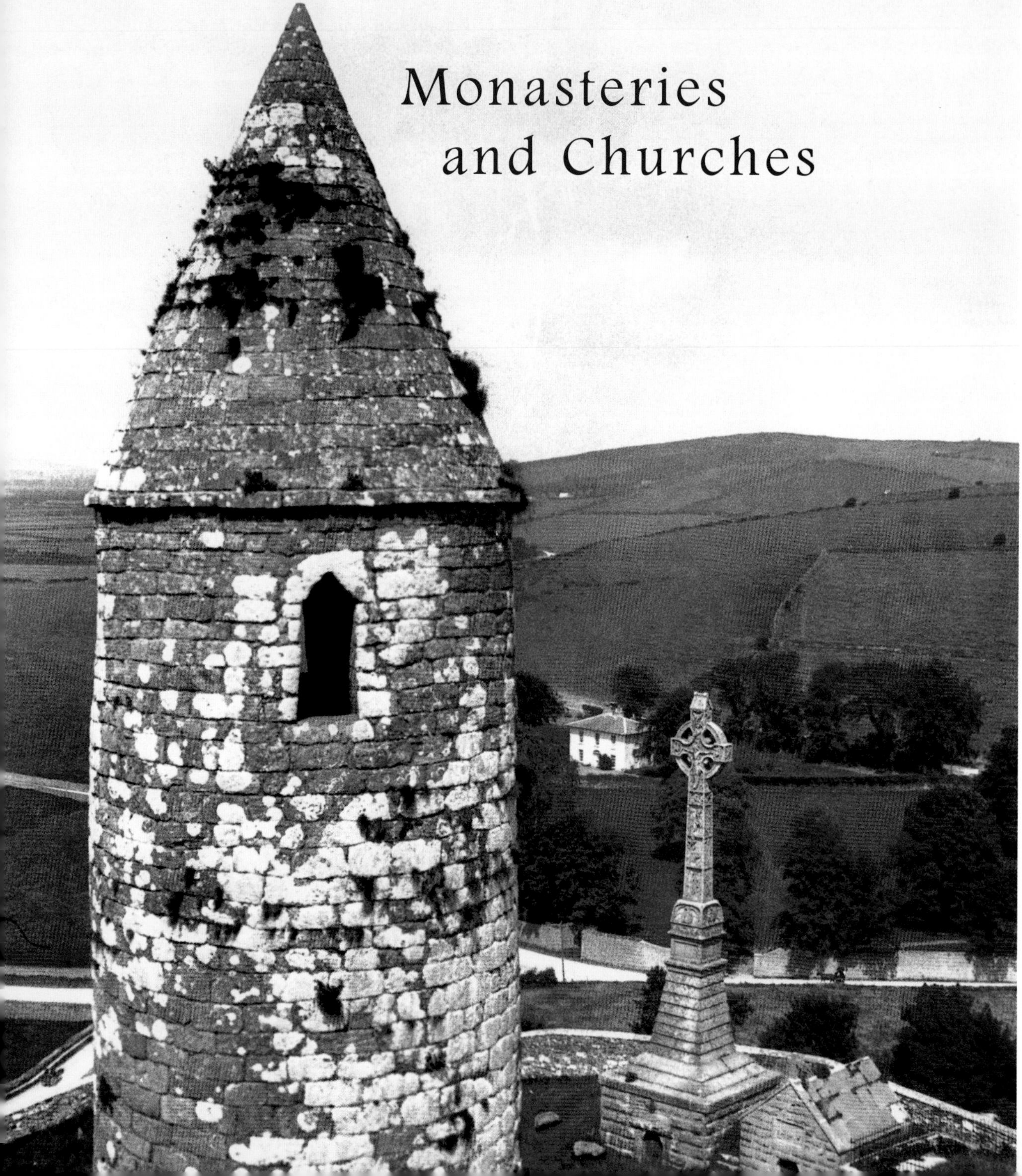

Opposite page: The Rock of Cashel (1931). The conical cap of the Round Tower has been repaired recently, having been struck by lightning. Built in the tenth century, it is one of the tallest in Ireland. The Celtic Cross is not an ancient one: it is a nineteenth-century monument to the Scully family which was struck by lightning and semi-demolished shortly after this photograph was taken.

The stone roof of Cormac's Chapel on the Rock of Cashel (1926). The two-storey roof was built in 1127 and is often compared to those at St Doulagh's, Malahide, and at St Columba's House, Kells.

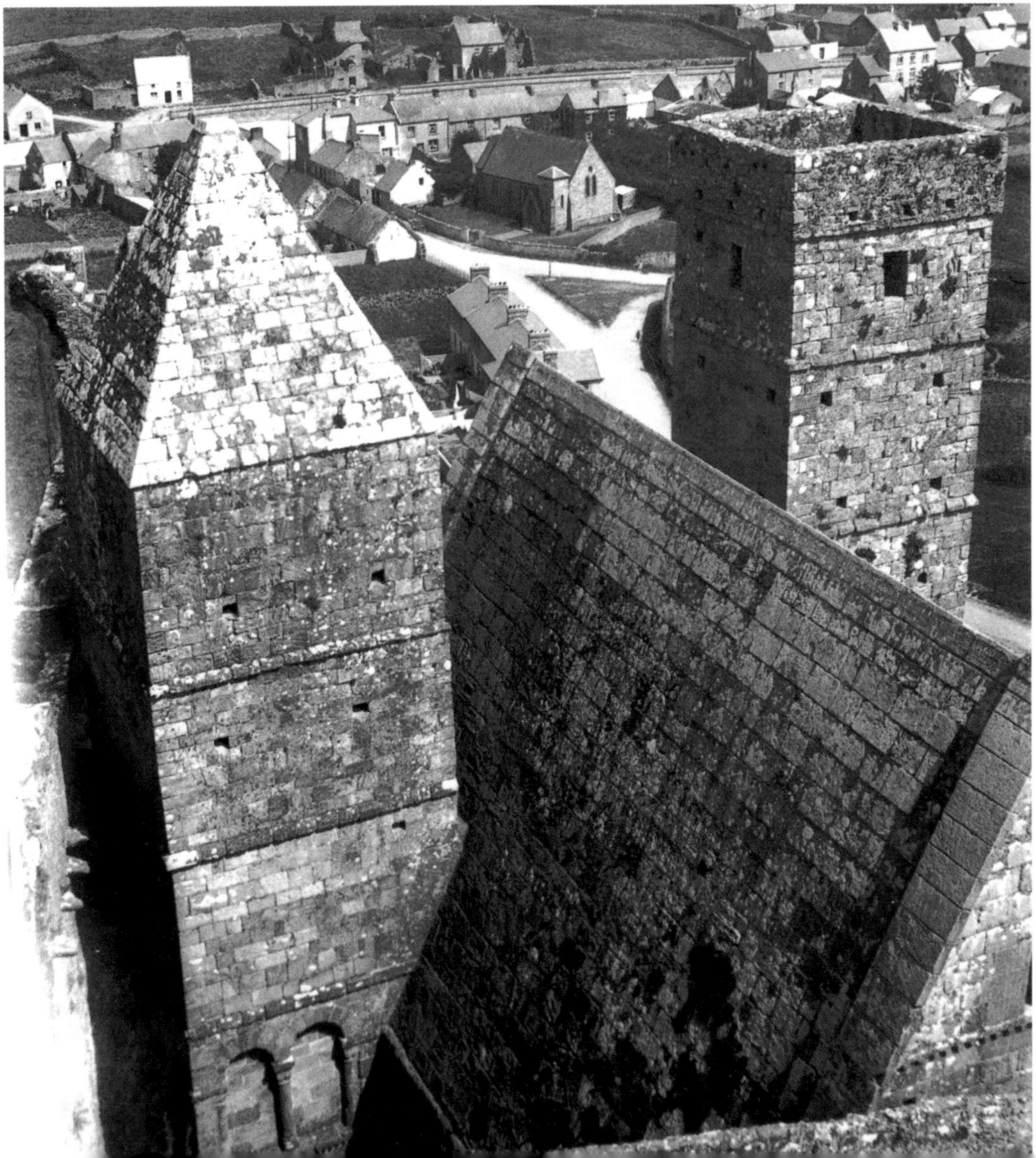

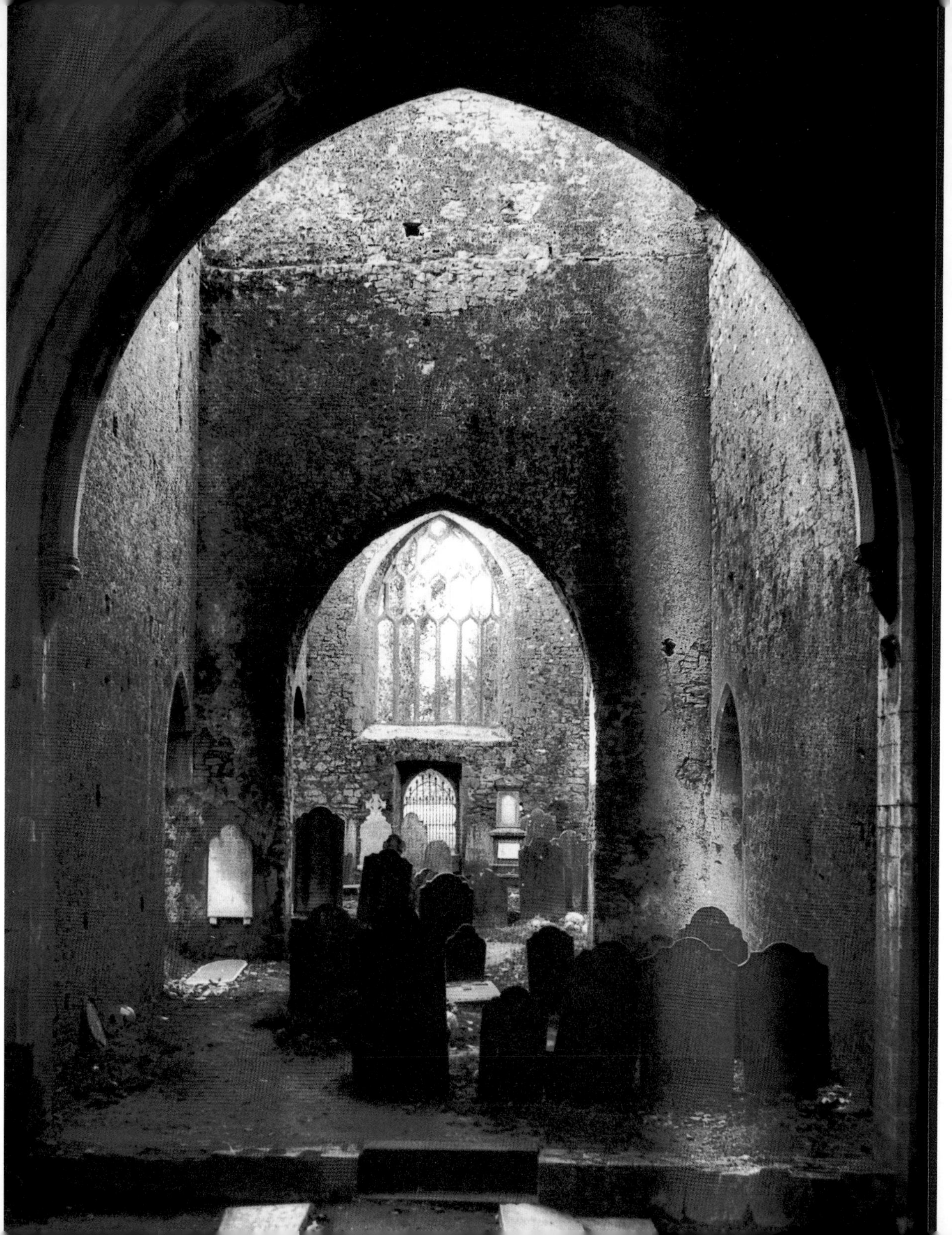

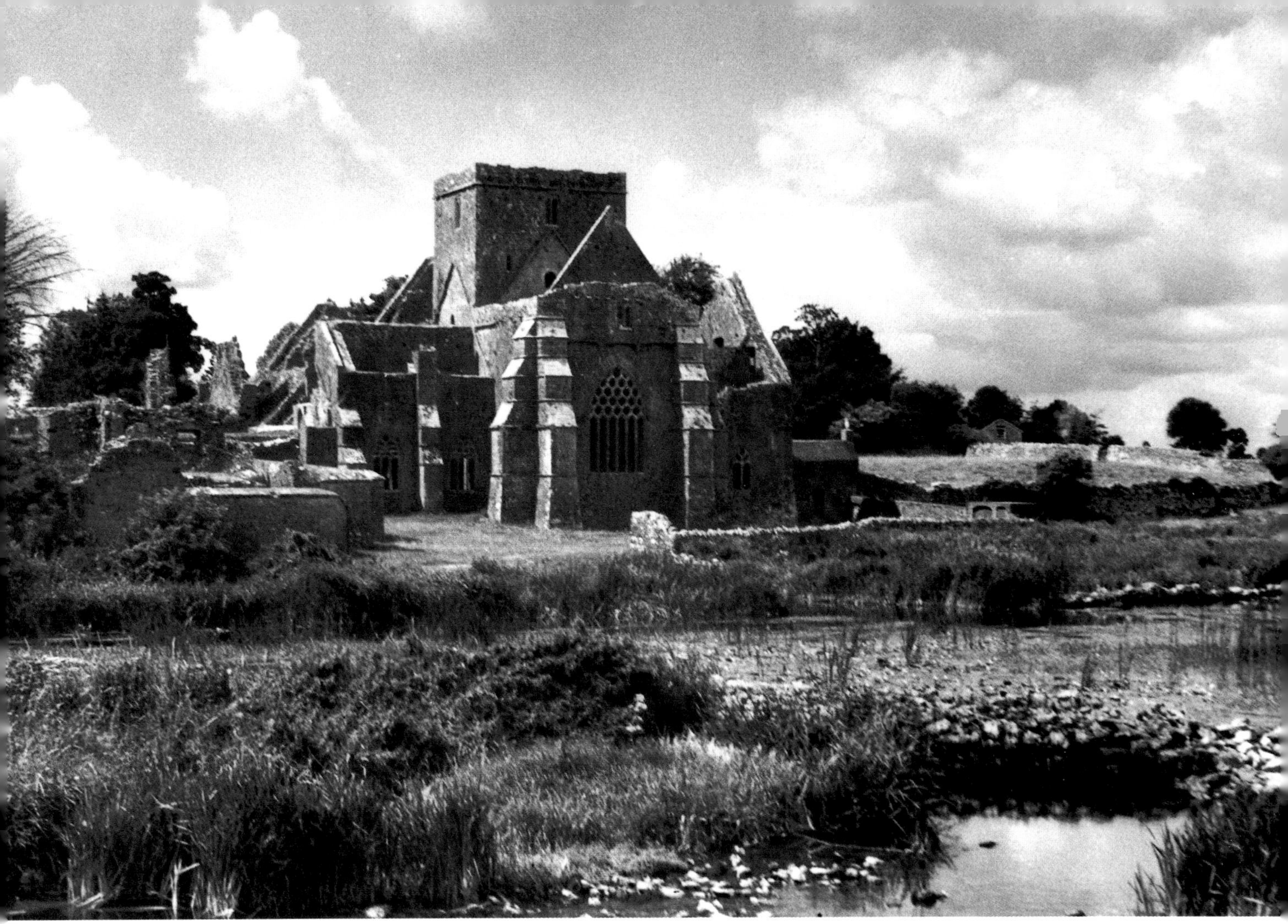

Holy Cross Abbey, viewed from across the River Suir using an early telephoto lens (1941). The abbey was founded in 1169 and was originally Benedictine. In 1180 it was given to the Cistercians by Donal Mór O'Brien.

Opposite page: The interior of Holy Cross Abbey (1941). This ruined church was re-roofed and beautifully restored in 1975 under the auspices of Archbishop Morris of Cashel & Emly.

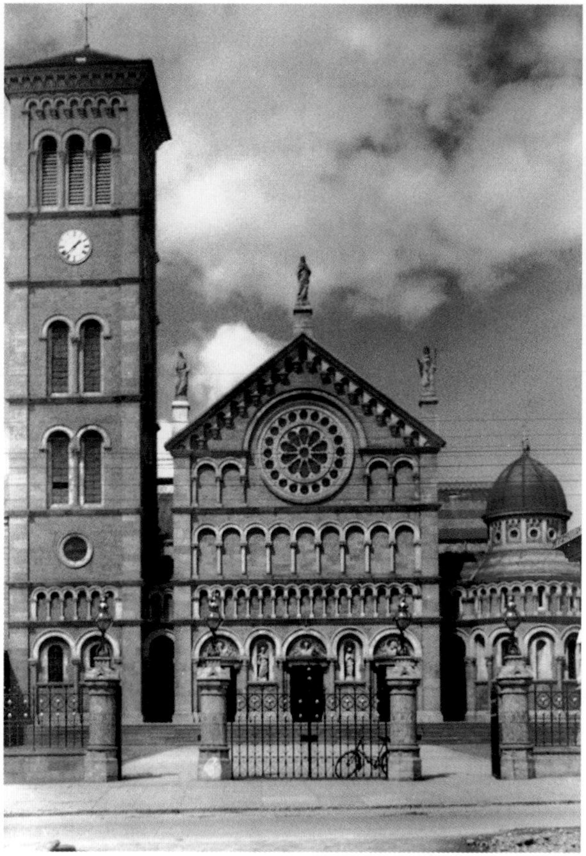

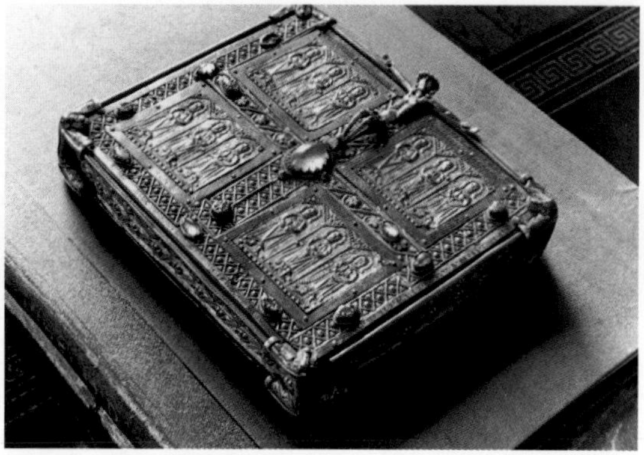

Above: The Book Shrine of St Caillin at St Patrick's College, Thurles (1944). The gem-encrusted, golden cover was for the Book of Fenagh which was kept in the library here for many years before being presented to the diocese of Ardagh and Clonmacnois.

Left: The Cathedral of the Assumption, Thurles (1937). The building was consecrated in 1879.

Opposite page: Interior of the Cathedral at Thurles showing the high altar and part of the beautifully decorated nave (1937).

Wall carvings and statues at the Rock of Cashel (1930). The statues represent the twelve apostles; the carvings of the dragons lead one to suspect a Welsh influence.

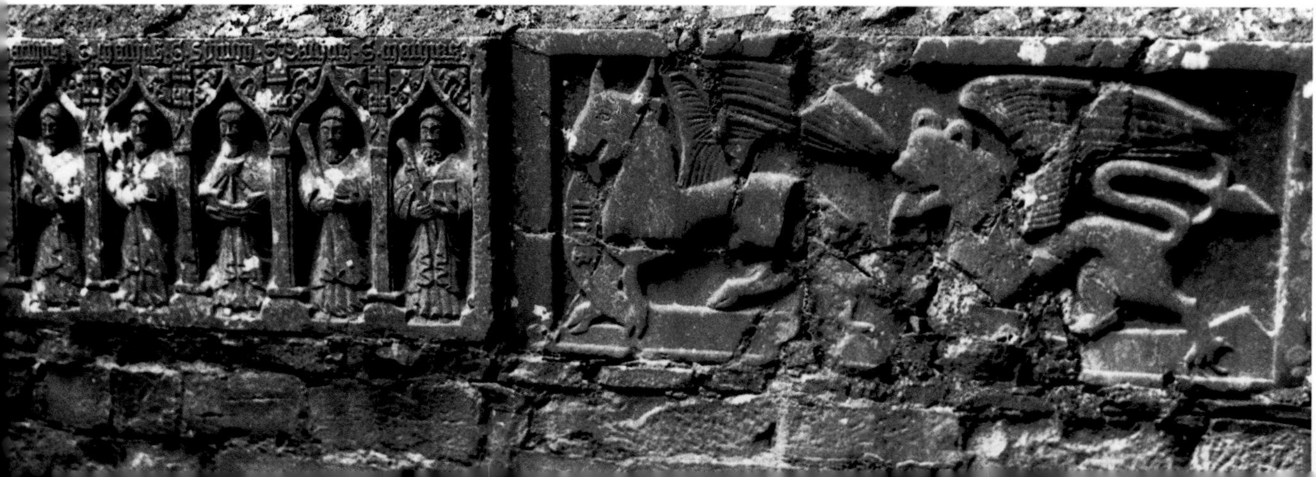

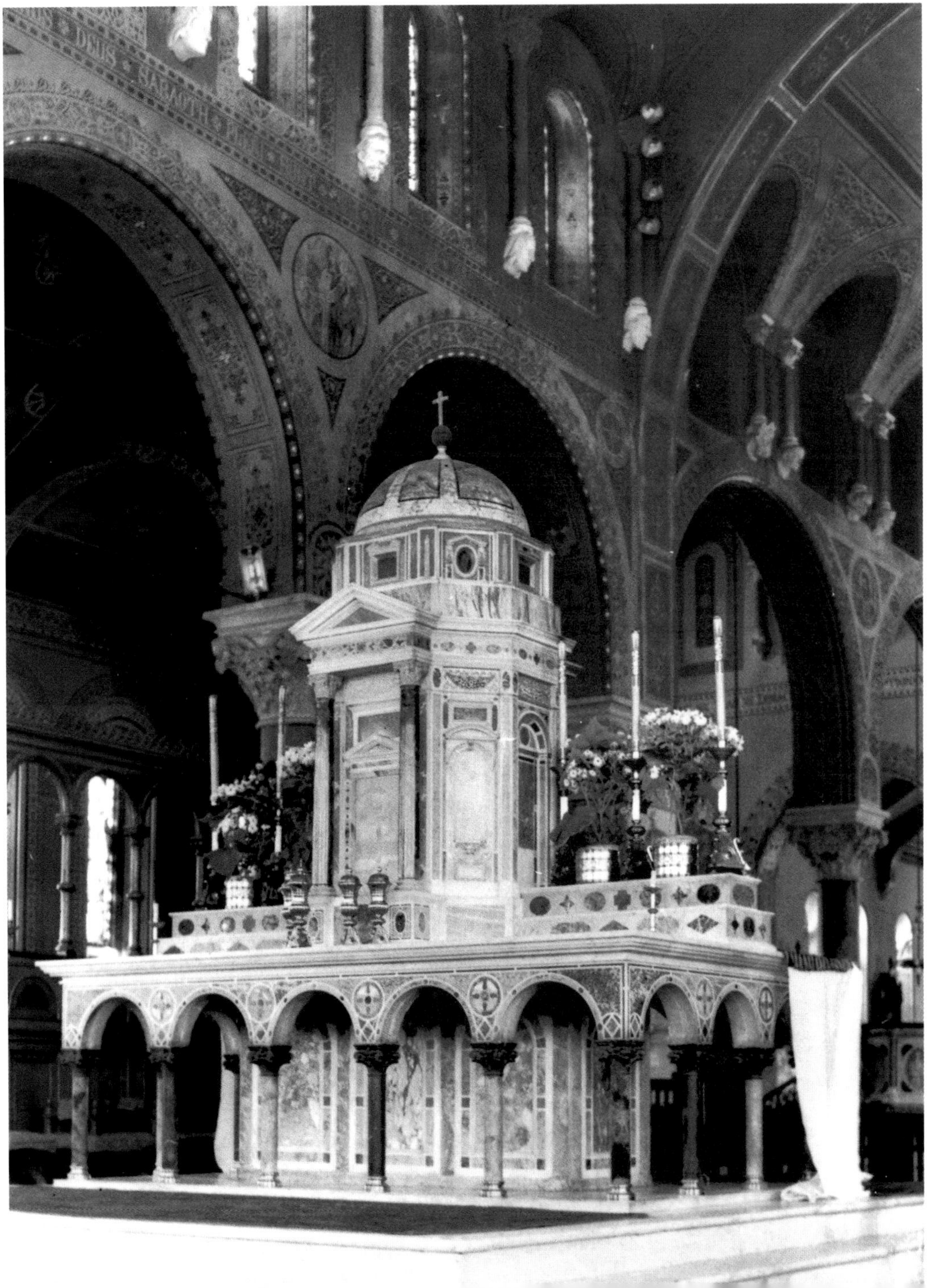

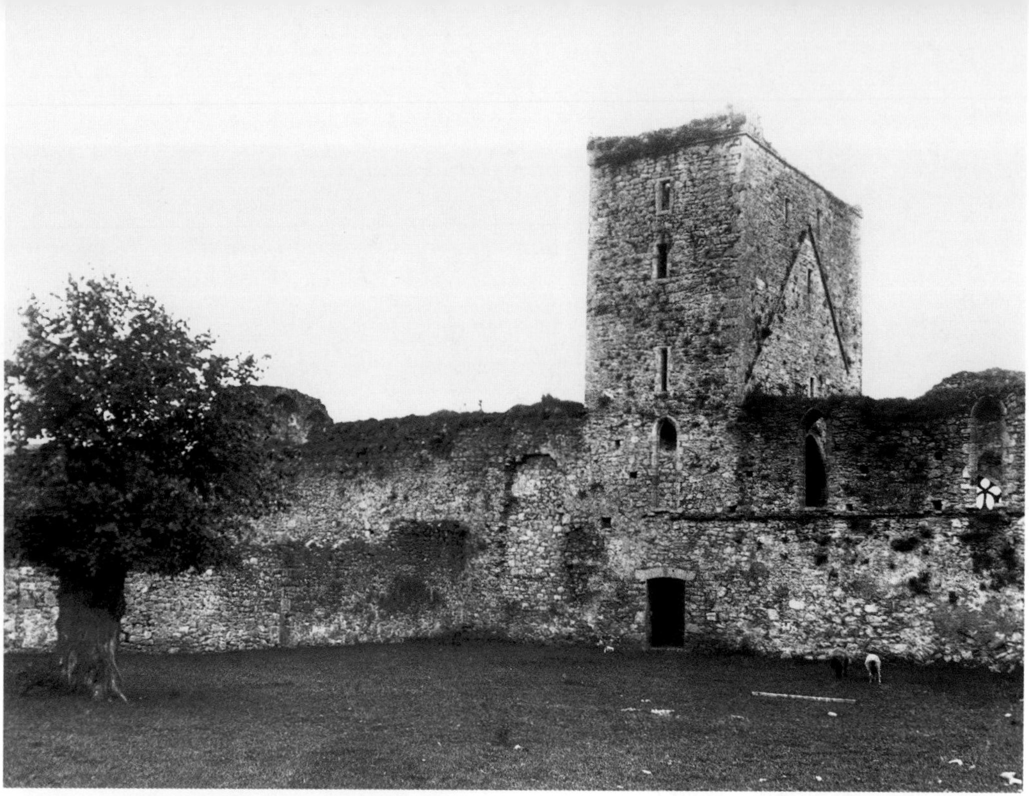

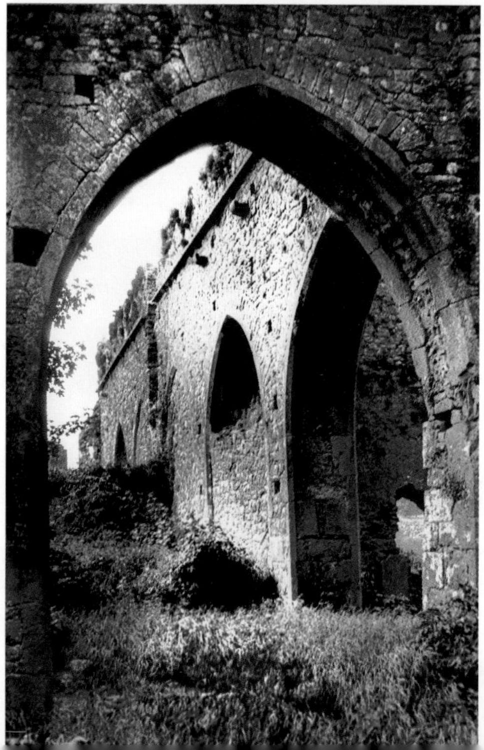

Above: Hore Abbey, near Cashel (1930). The Benedictines came here from Glastonbury at the close of the twelfth century but were replaced by the Cistercians in 1272.

Left: St Dominic's Abbey, Cashel (1930). In fact a priory, this was one of the first Dominican churches to be built in Ireland. It was founded by Arcbishop MacKelly who died in 1252. General Chapters of the Dominicans were held here in 1289 and 1307.

Opposite page: 'Grandpa's Rosary', in the hills above Tipperary town (1940).

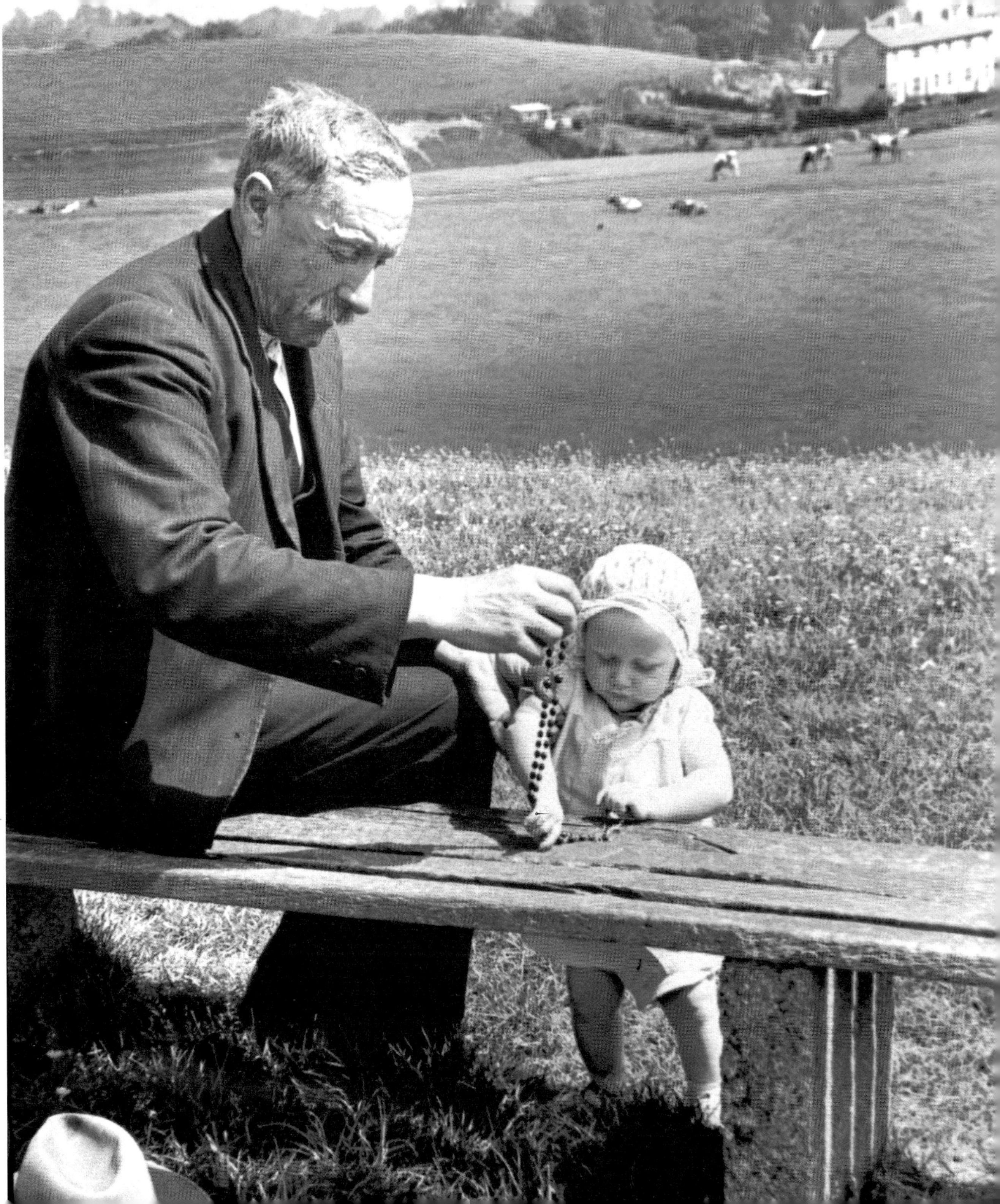

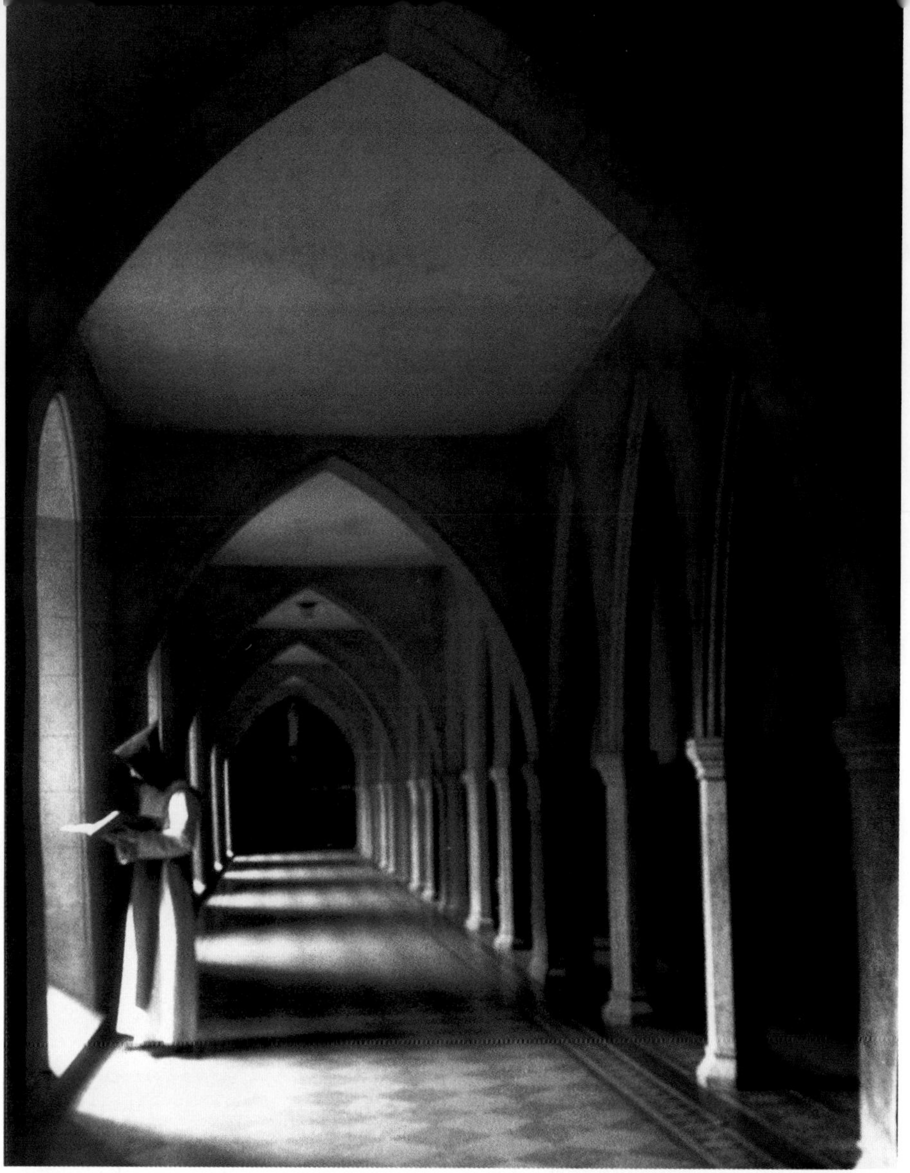

'Elected Silence.' A Cistercian monk photographed on the south side of the cloisters at Mount Saint Joseph's, Roscrea (1930).

Opposite page: Mount Saint Joseph's, Roscrea (1930). A close-up of the choir and the monks' choir-stalls.

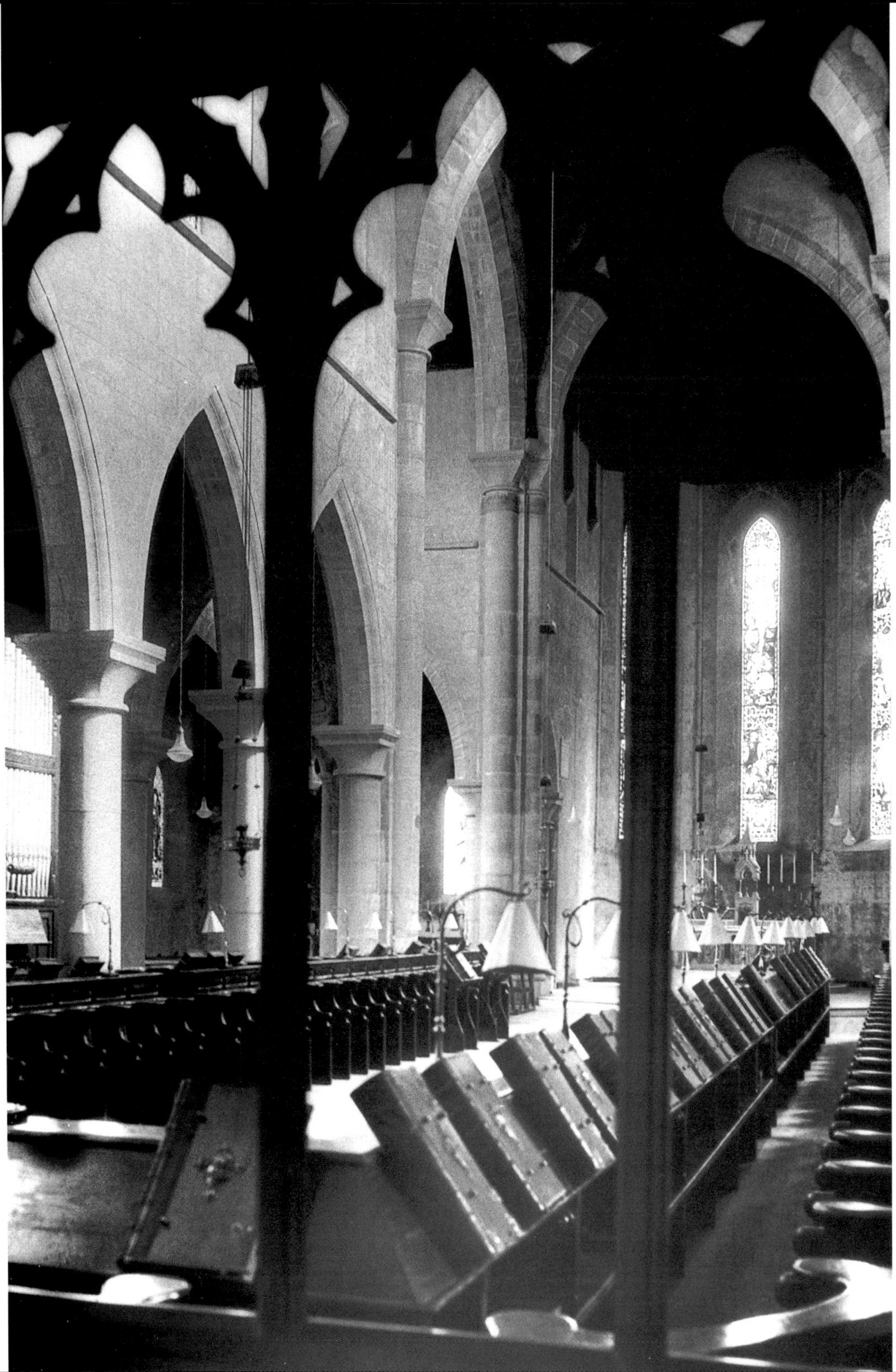

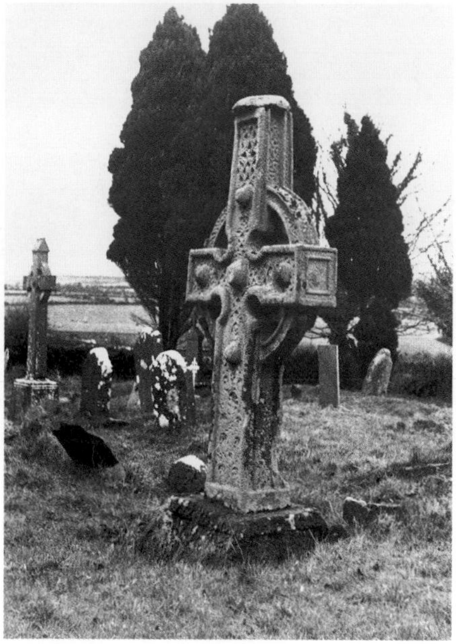

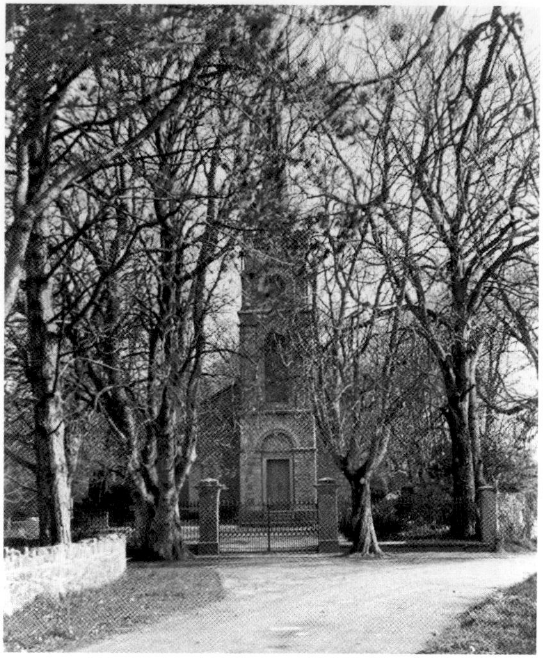

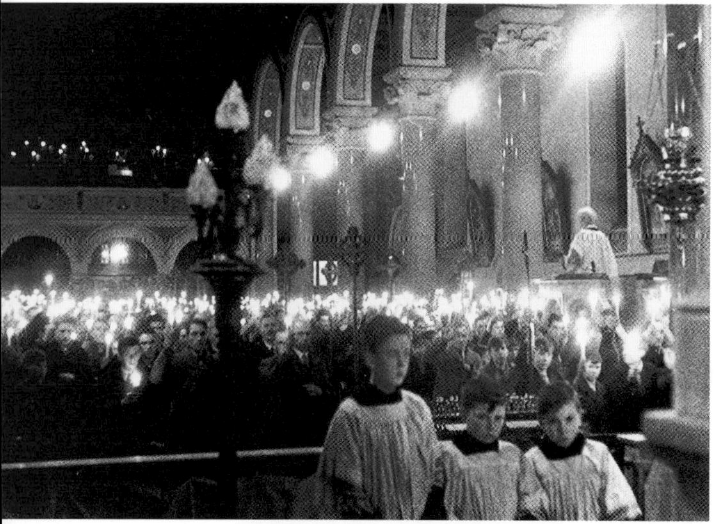

Above left: The High Cross at Kilbenny (1936). The ancient Celtic crosses at Kilbenny are quite unusual because of the height of the stone above the cross-piece.

Above right: The Church of Ireland near Carrick-on-Suir, on the road to Kilmaganny (1944).

Left: The candle-lit closing of the 'mission' preached by Fr Michael Garraghy, S.J., at Carrick-on-Suir in 1936.

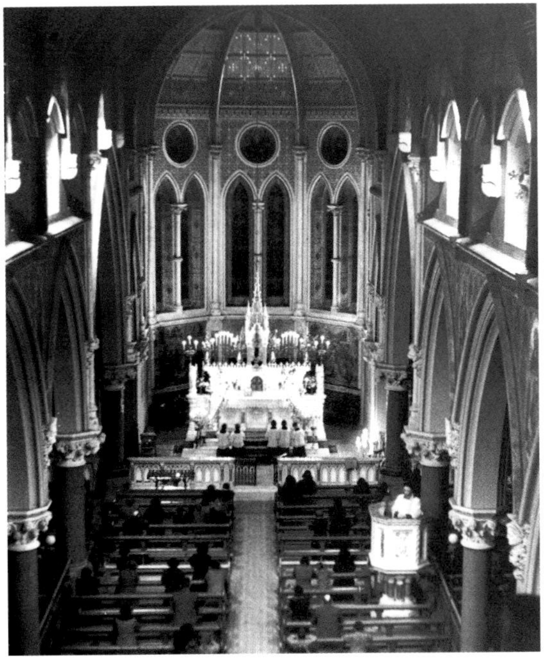

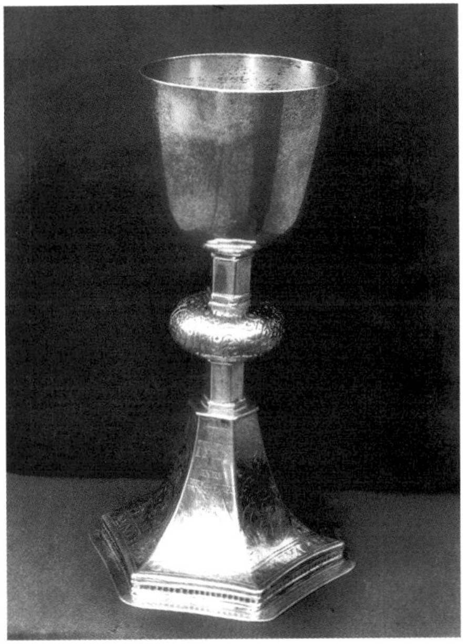

Above left: Worshippers observing the Holy Hour at the Church of the Sacred Heart, Templemore (1937).

Above right: This medieval chalice belonging to Holy Cross Abbey was found in the River Owenacurra near Lisgoold, County Cork (1930).

Right: St Cronan's Cross, Roscrea (1943). A twelfth-century High Cross featuring Christ and interlacing Celtic designs on the west face.

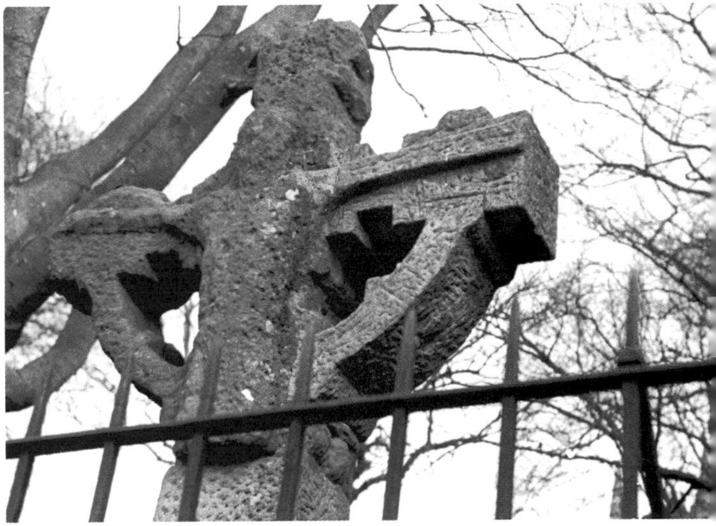

People

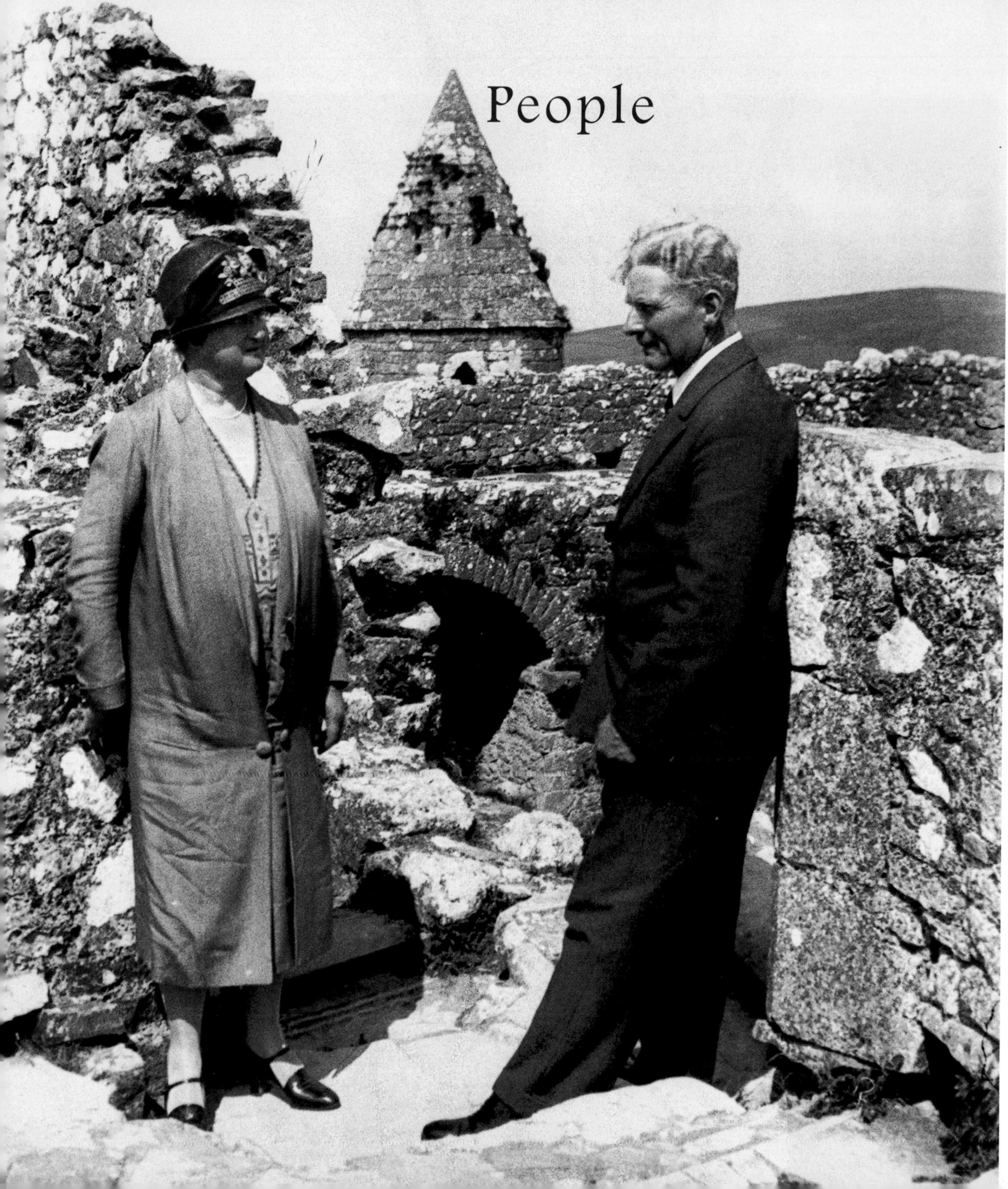

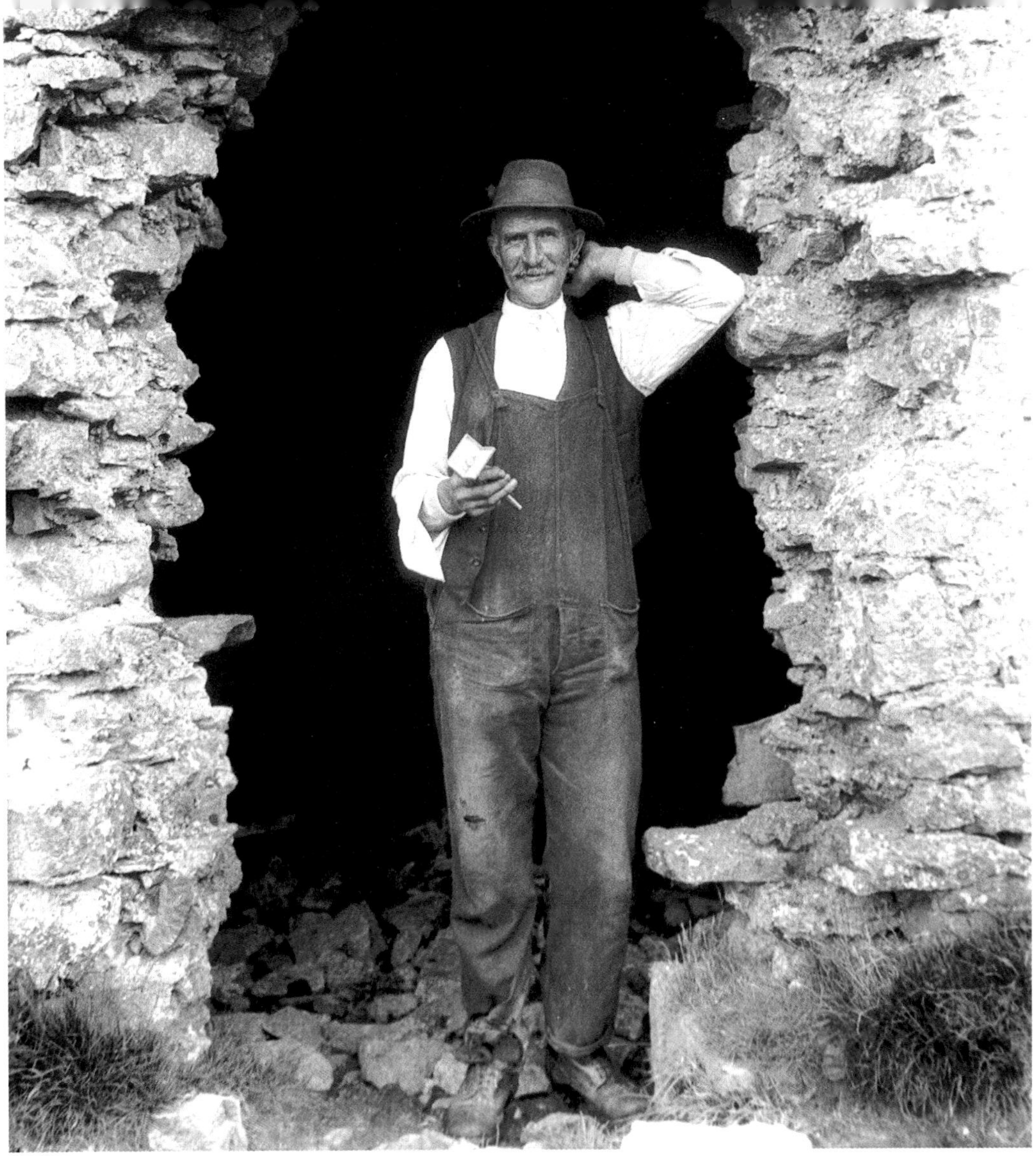

Tom Ryan, Custodian, at Kilcooley Abbey (1931). An employee of the Barker-Ponsonby family who own the nearby house, Tom showed Father Browne around the Cistercian monastery that was founded in 1182.

Opposite page: Mrs Bourke of Melbourne chats with the custodian atop the Rock of Cashel (1926).

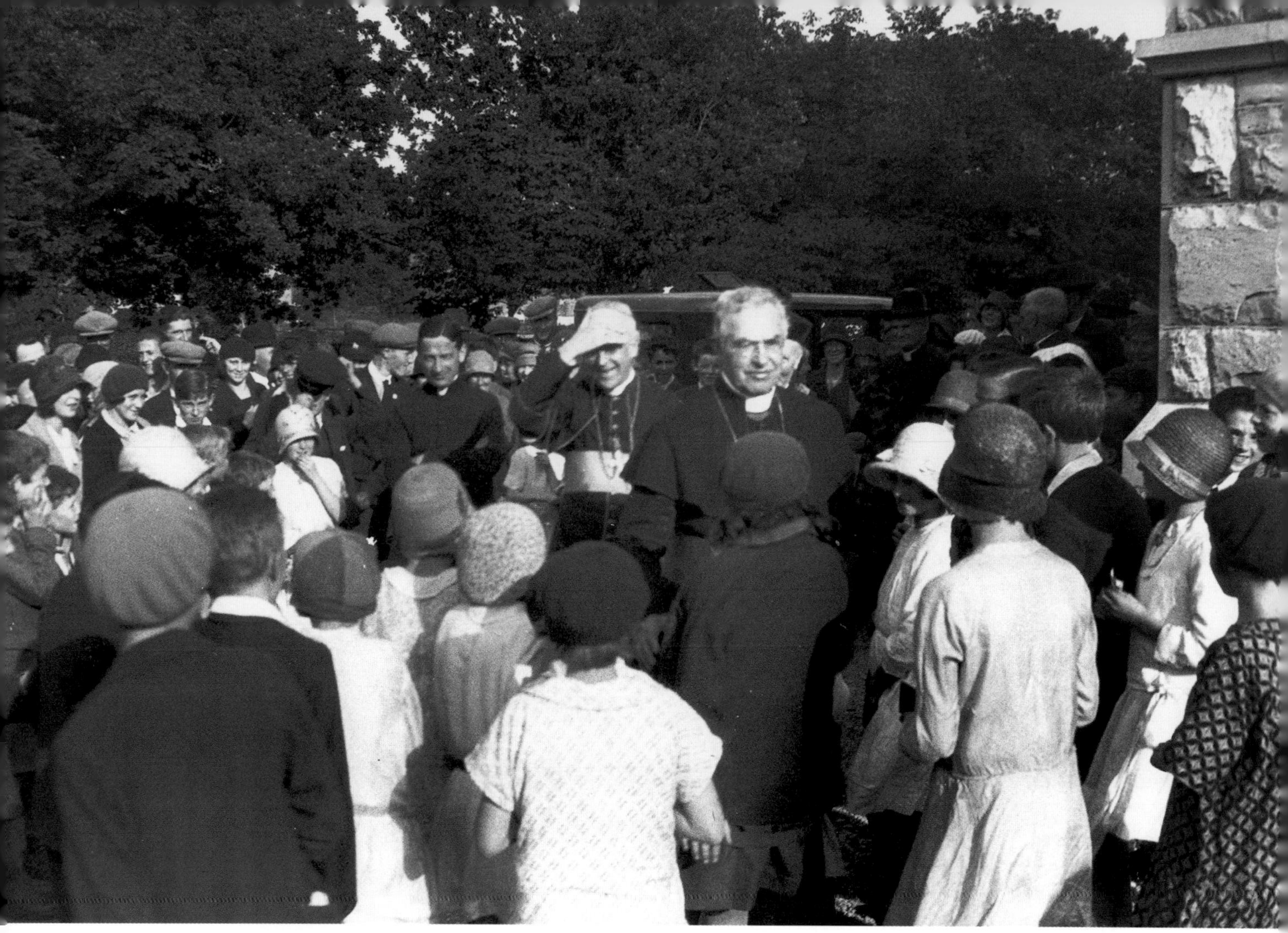

The Papal Nuncio, Dr Paschal Robinson, being greeted by the populace at Nenagh in 1930.

Opposite page: Peter McDermot of Terryglass (1935).

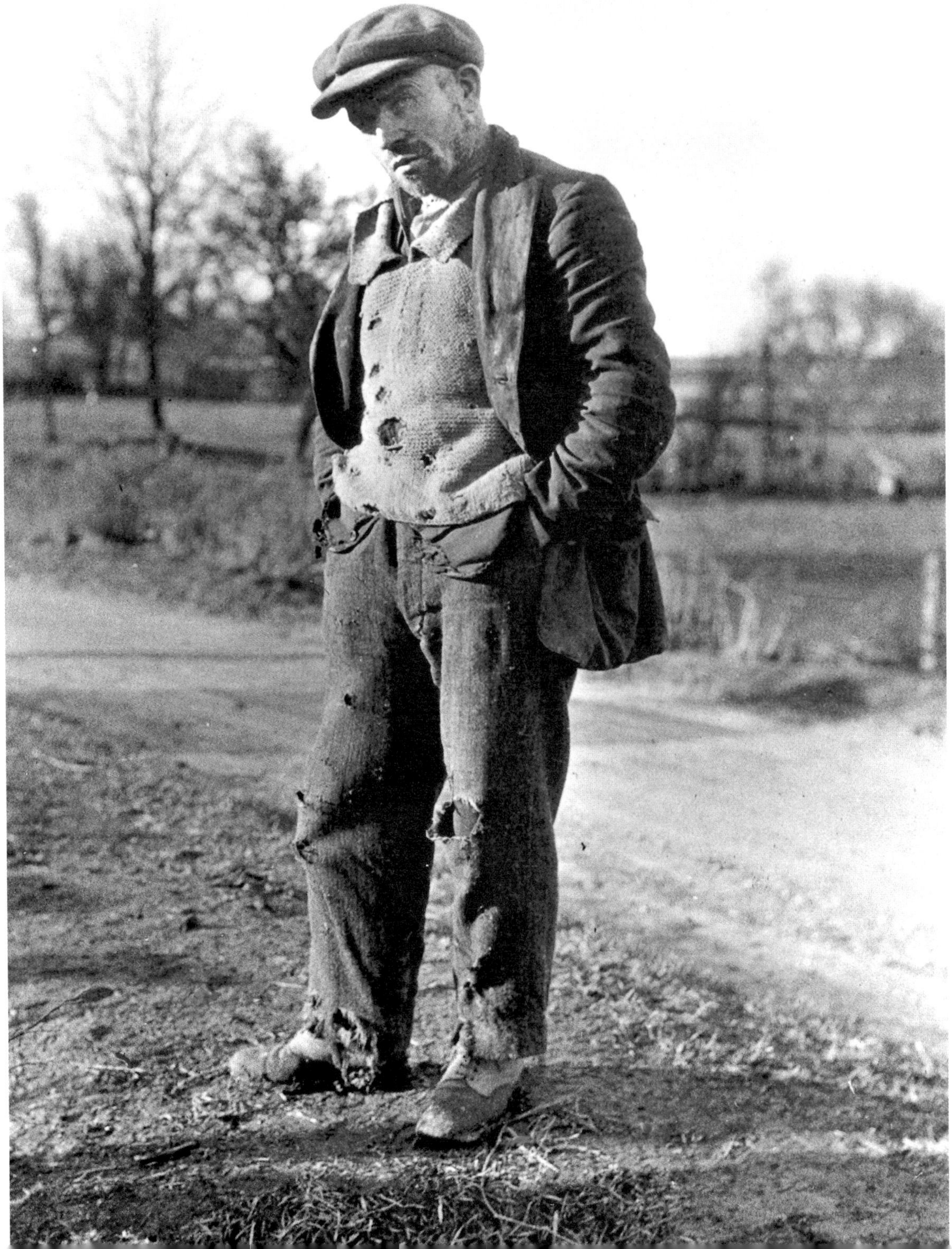

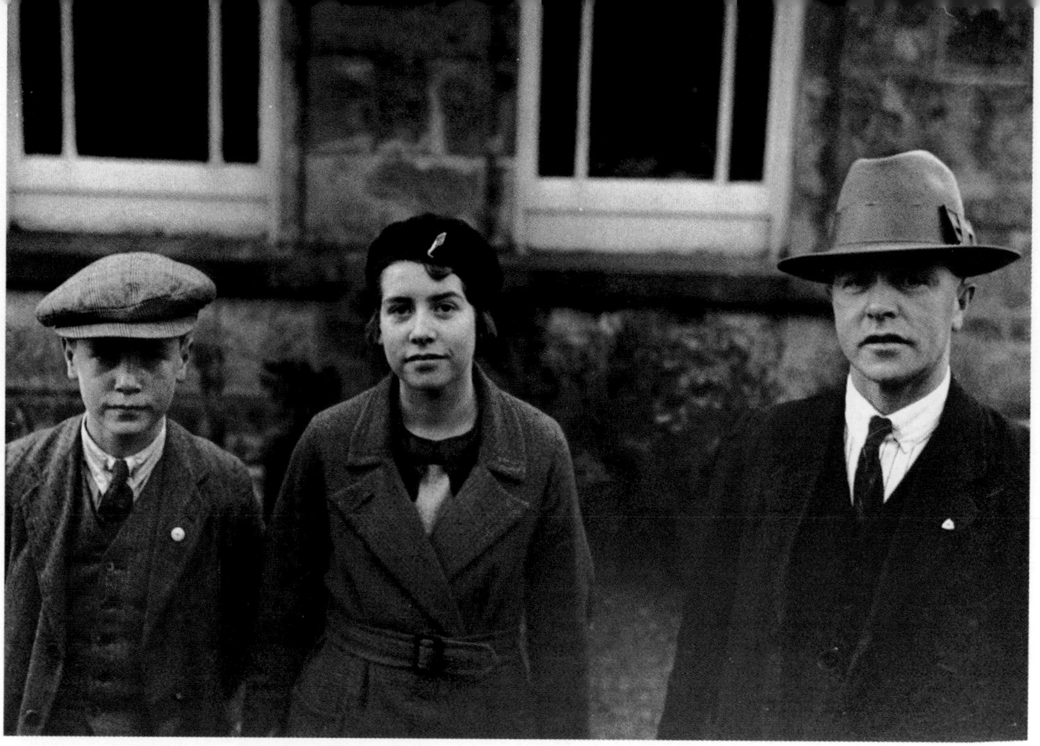

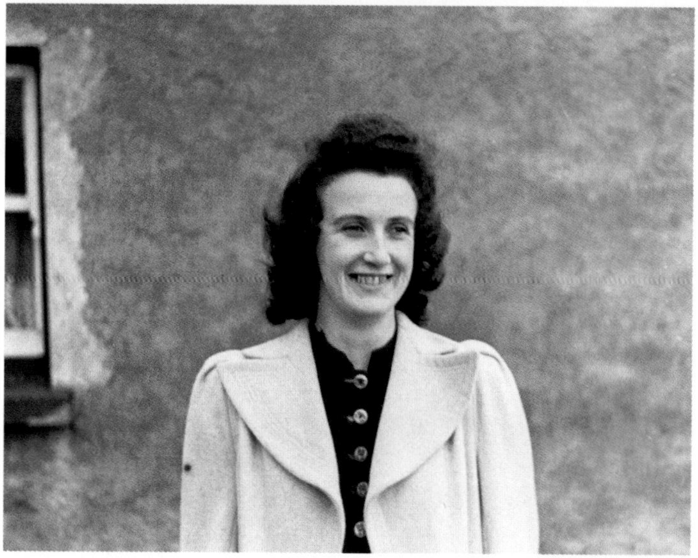

Above: Sergeant Moyney V.C. and his children, near Nenagh (1938). Father Browne had served with the Sergeant in the Irish Guards during World War I.

Left: Miss Monty Lonergan at Kilcash (1945).

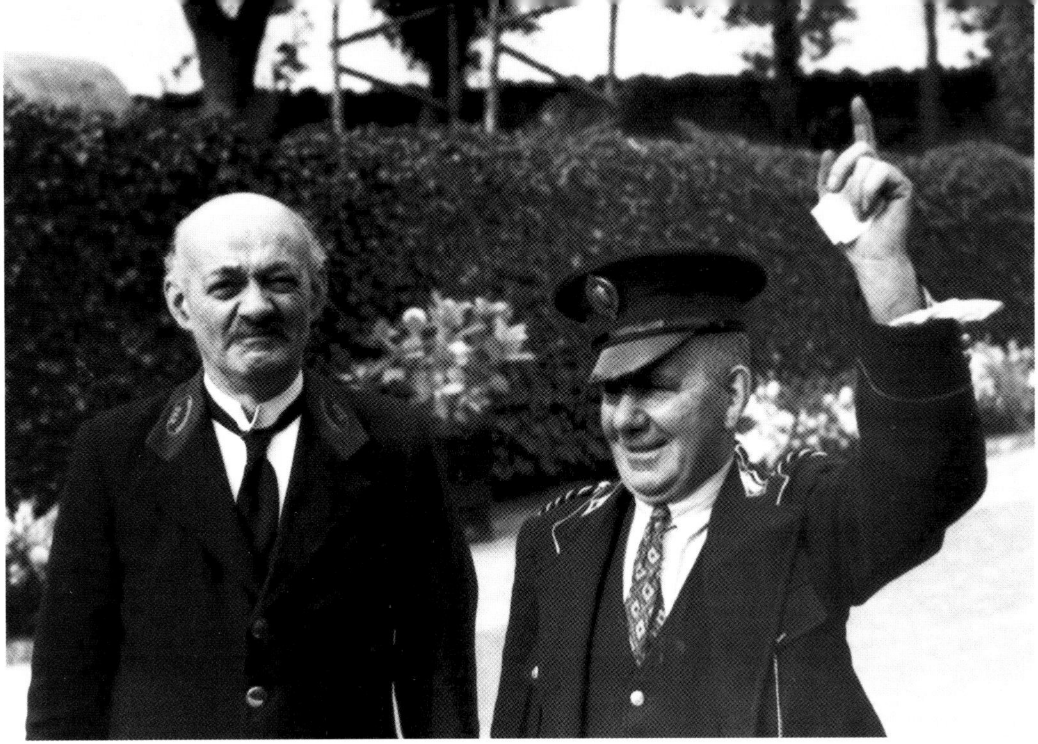

Above: 'Railway Personalities' (1940). F. Sullivan and B. McEvoy are photographed at Cloughjordan station.

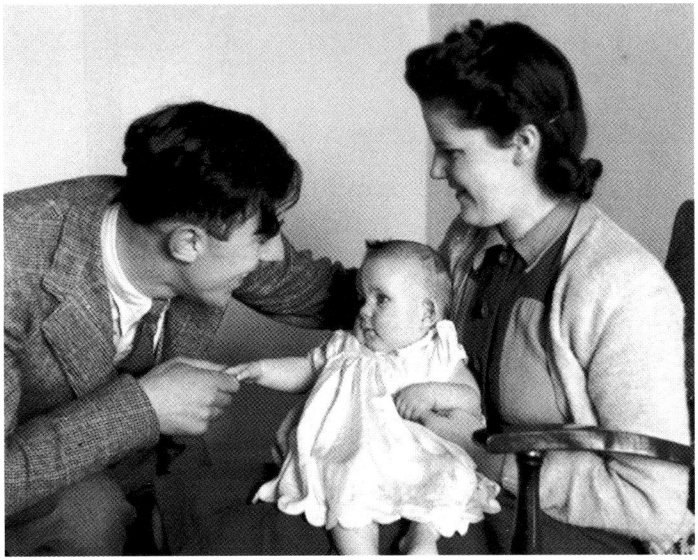

Right: Mr & Mrs R. Burke of Carrick-on-Suir play with the baby in November 1944.

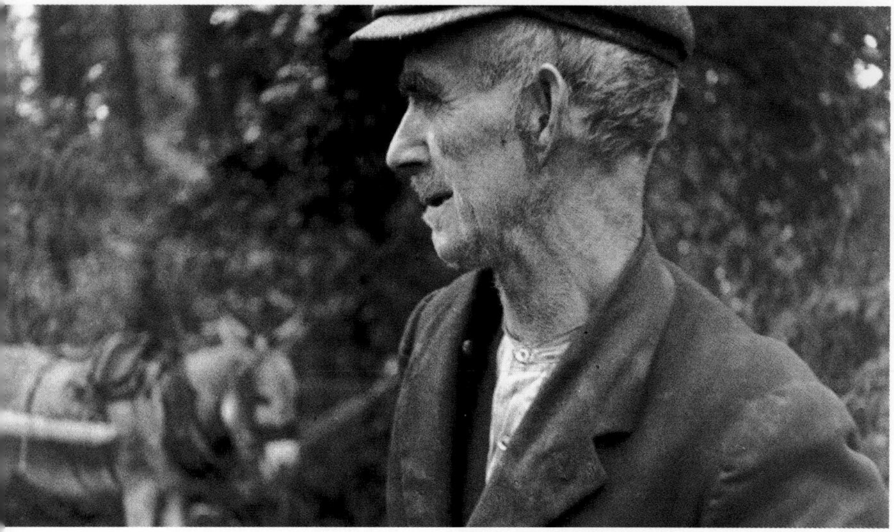

Left: 'The farmer and his pet' (1937). Taken on the road between Borrisoleigh and Templemore.

Below: Mr & Mrs Pat Davin framed in the doorway of their house in Carrick-on-Suir (1944).

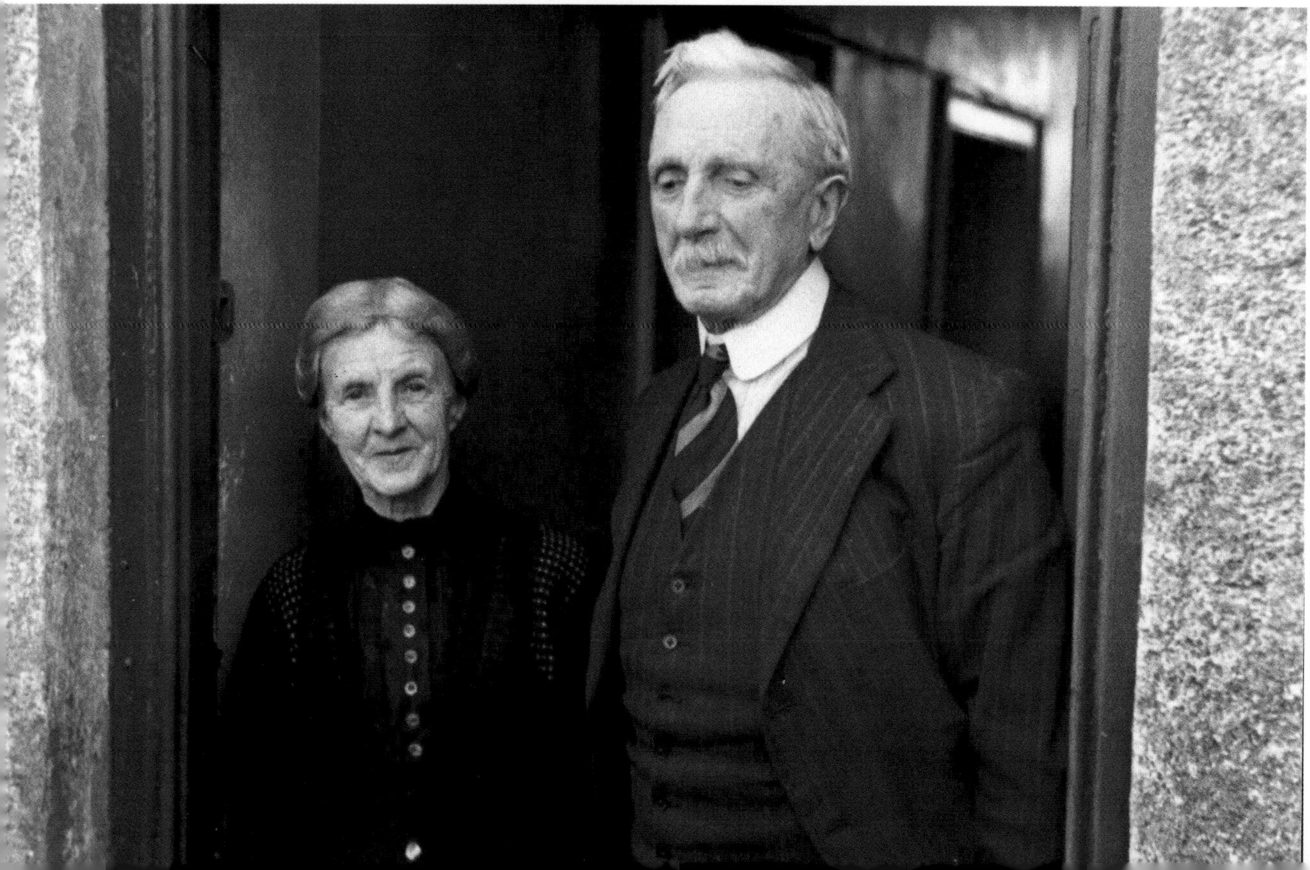

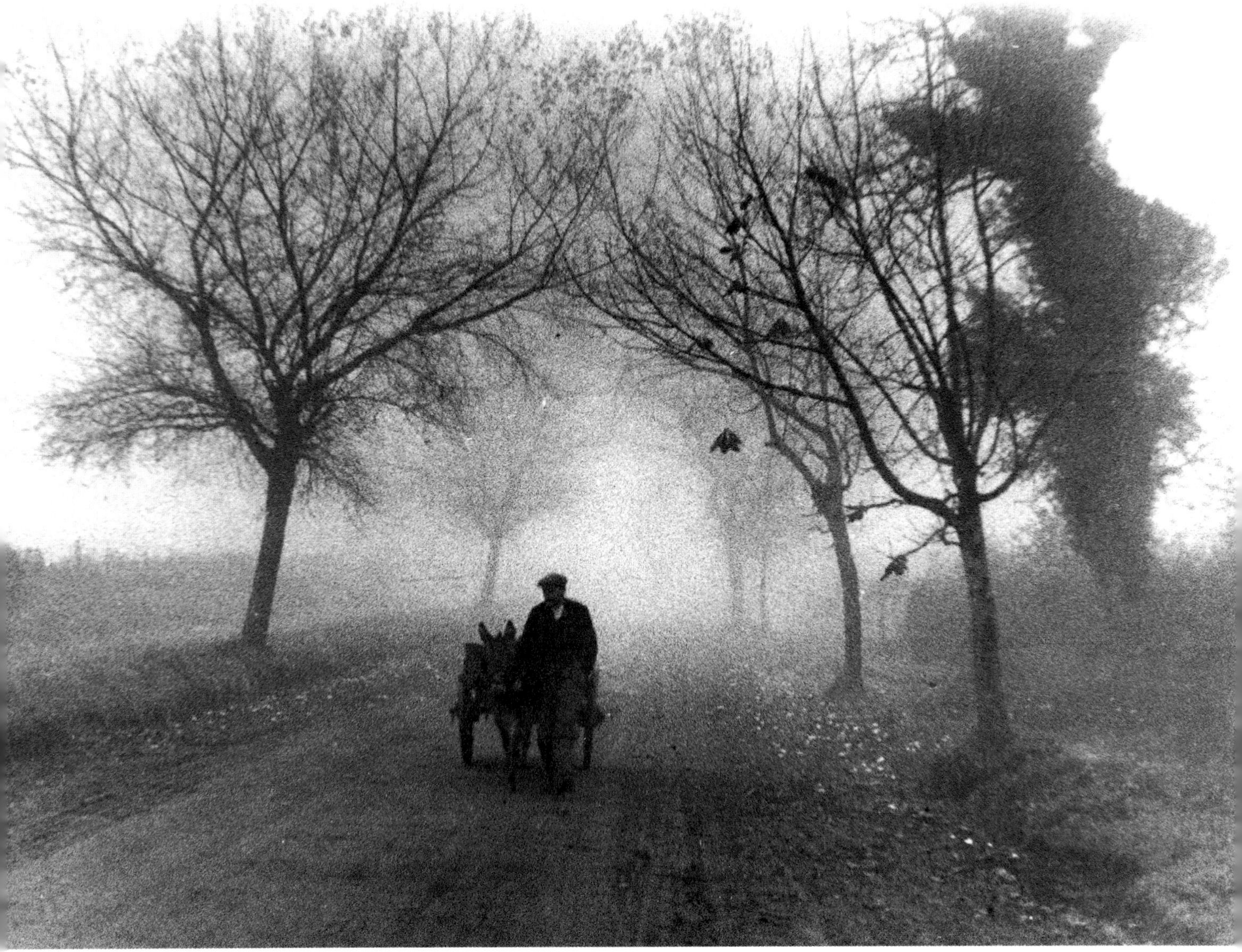

A farmer making his way home in the fog on the Borrisoleigh Road from Templemore (1937).

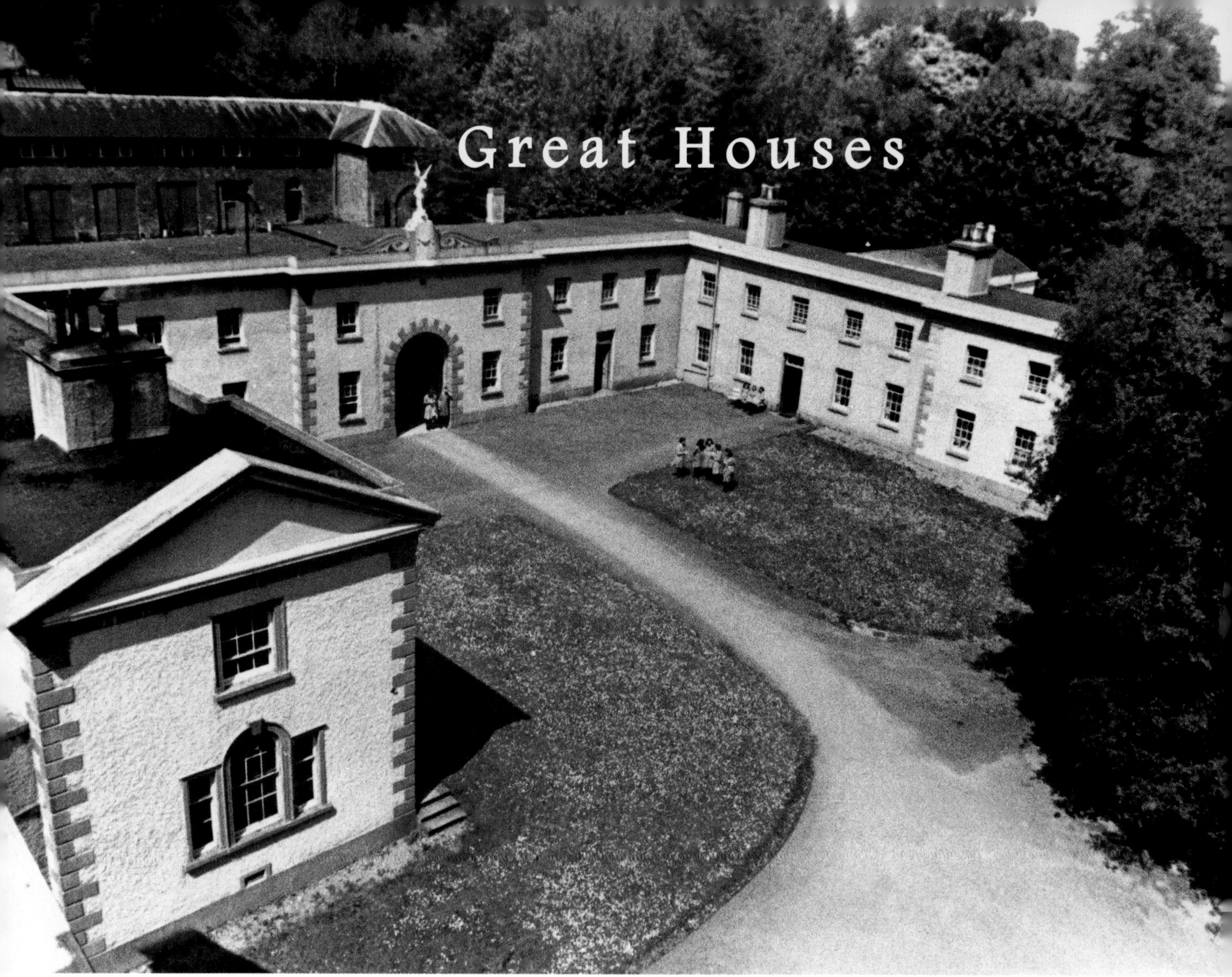

Great Houses

Dundrum House (1944). Rear view showing the buildings added in 1890 by the fourth Viscount Hawarden, who was the first (and last) Earl of Montalt.

Opposite page: Reflections in a Georgian room. An ornate old mirror at Mooresfort, near Lattin (1930).

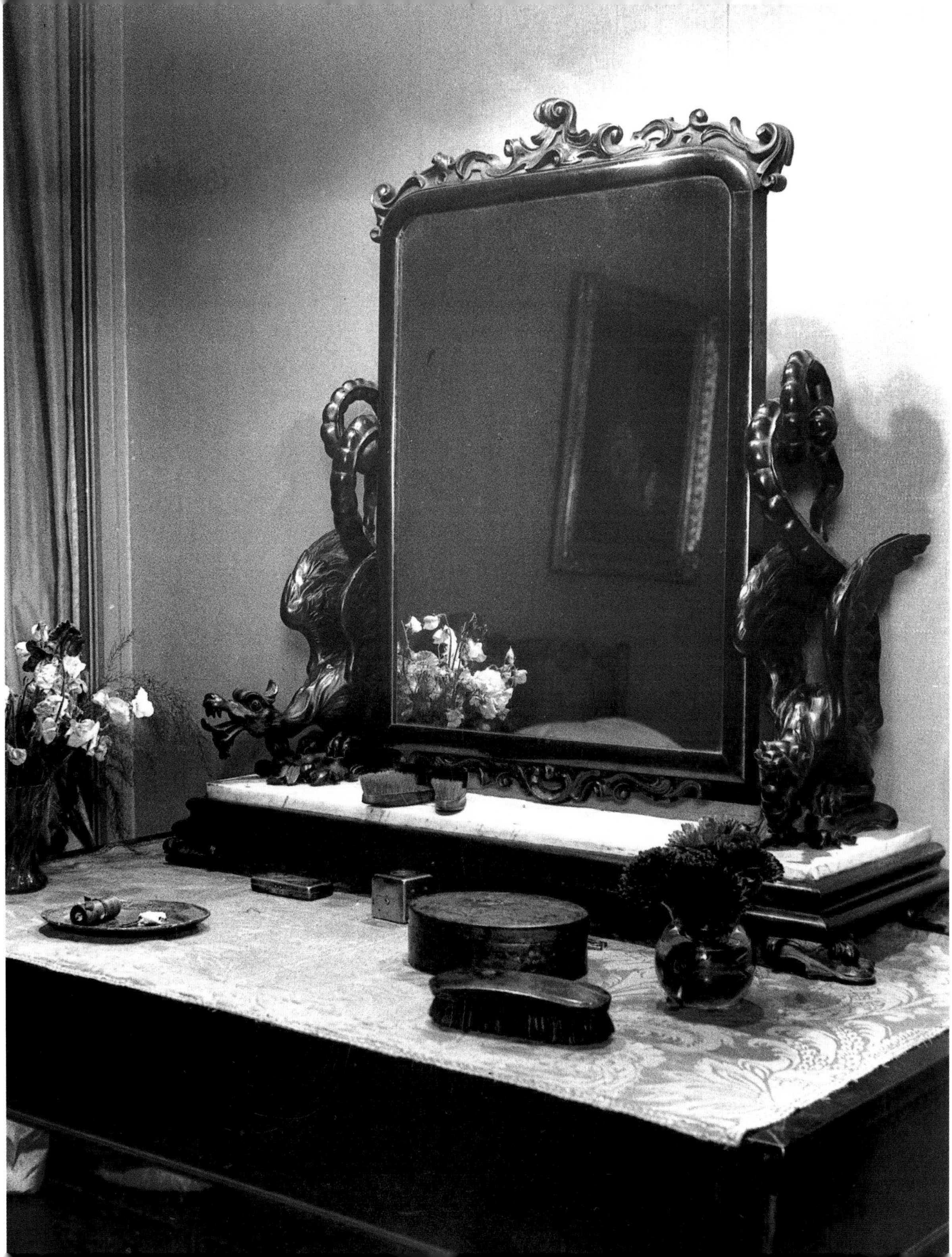

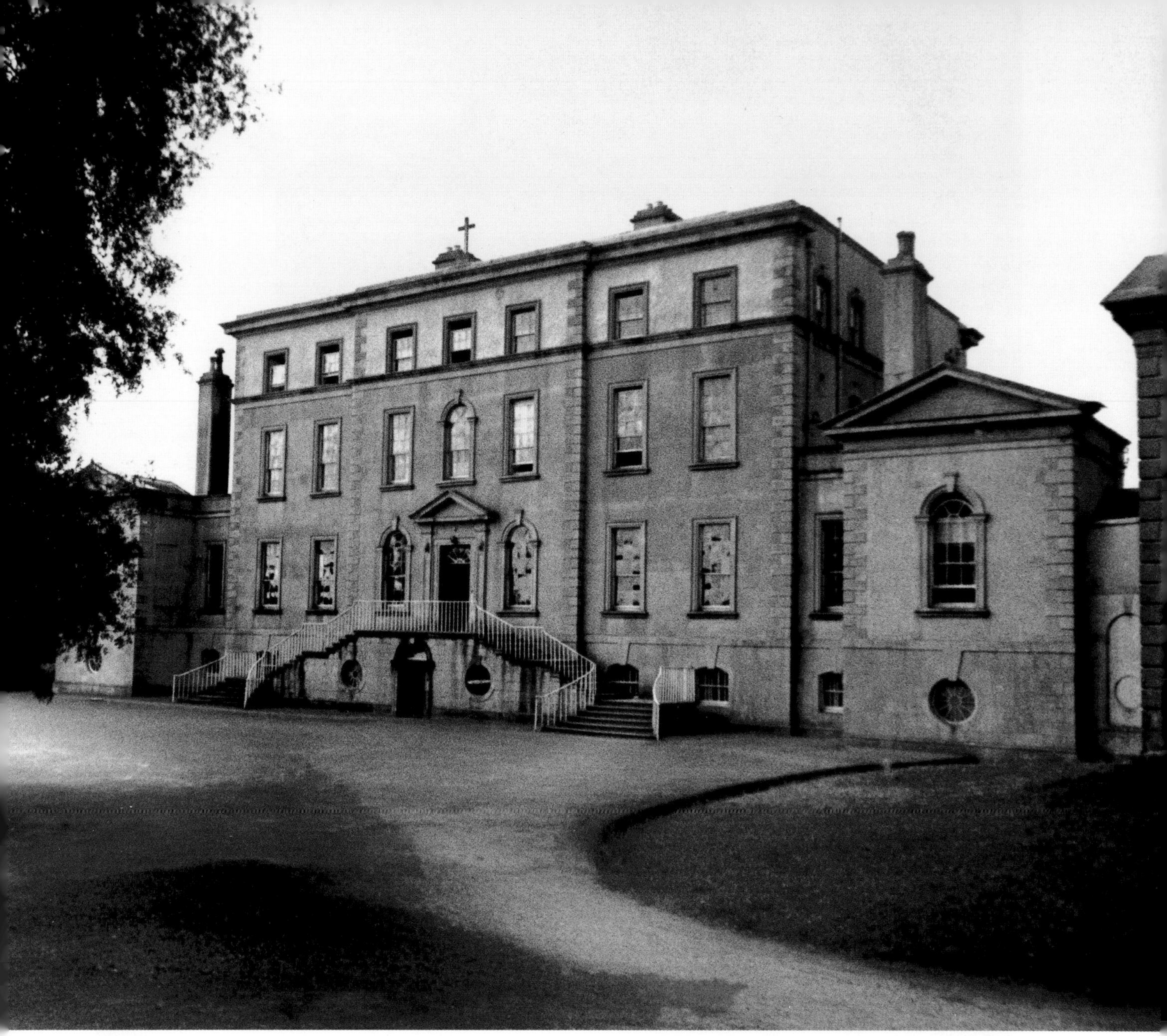

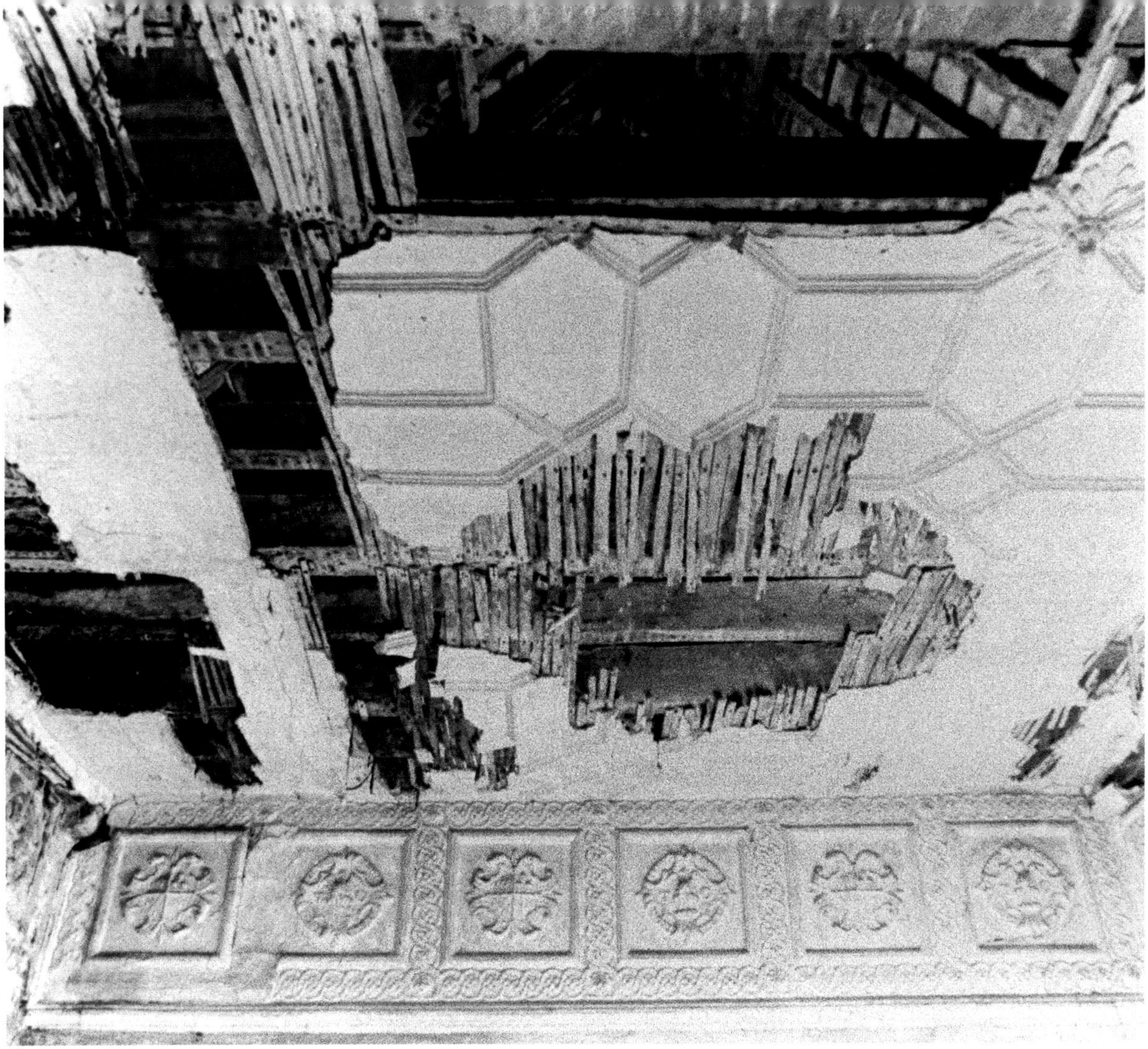

Ruined ceiling at Carrick-on-Suir Castle (1944). A reconstructed section of the ceiling now shows what the whole must have been like originally.

Opposite page: Dundrum House (1944). An eighteenth-century Palladian building, originally the home of the Maude family, the Viscounts Hawarden. This picture was taken from what is now the golf-course of the hotel that replaced the Presentation Convent.

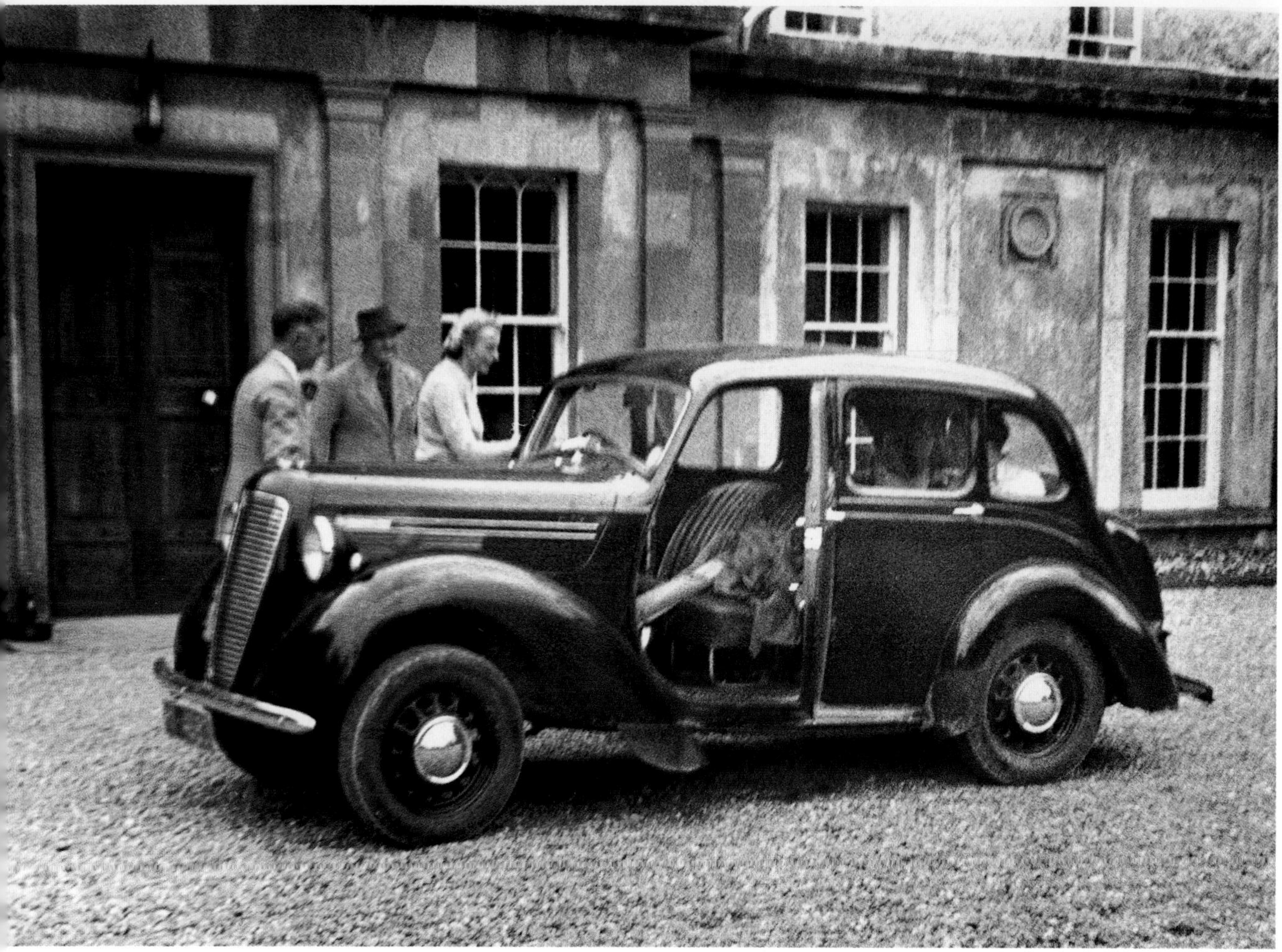

Guests arrive at Knocklofty House, the home of Lord and Lady Donoughmore (1948). The family name was Hely-Hutchinson and the house was built early in the eighteenth century. In 1985 it became the Knocklofty Country House & Leisure Centre.

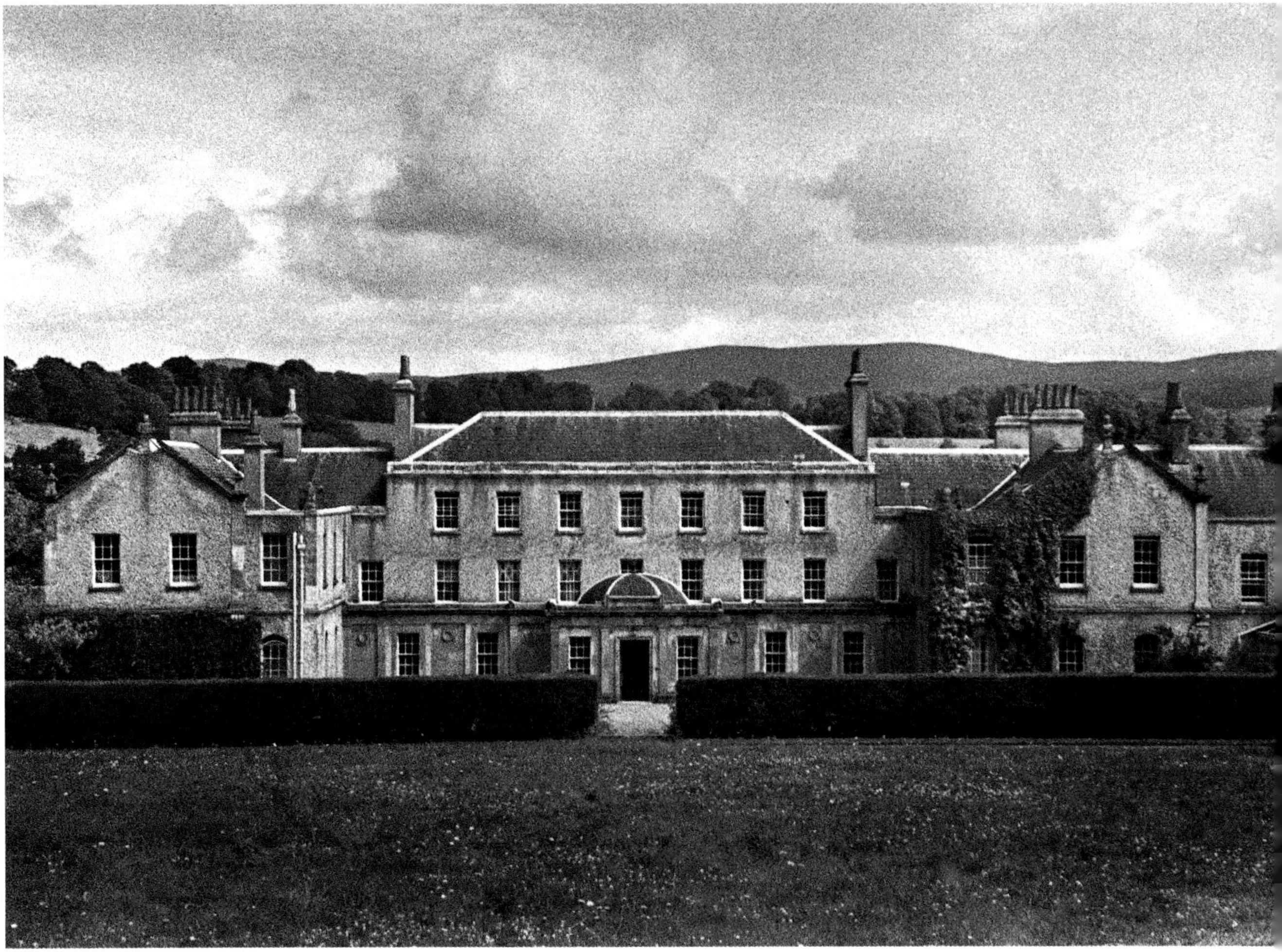

Overview of Knocklofty House showing the centre block of seven bays, with wings of two bays used as pediments surmounted by ornaments (1948). The two-storey flanking corridors are crowned with eagles.

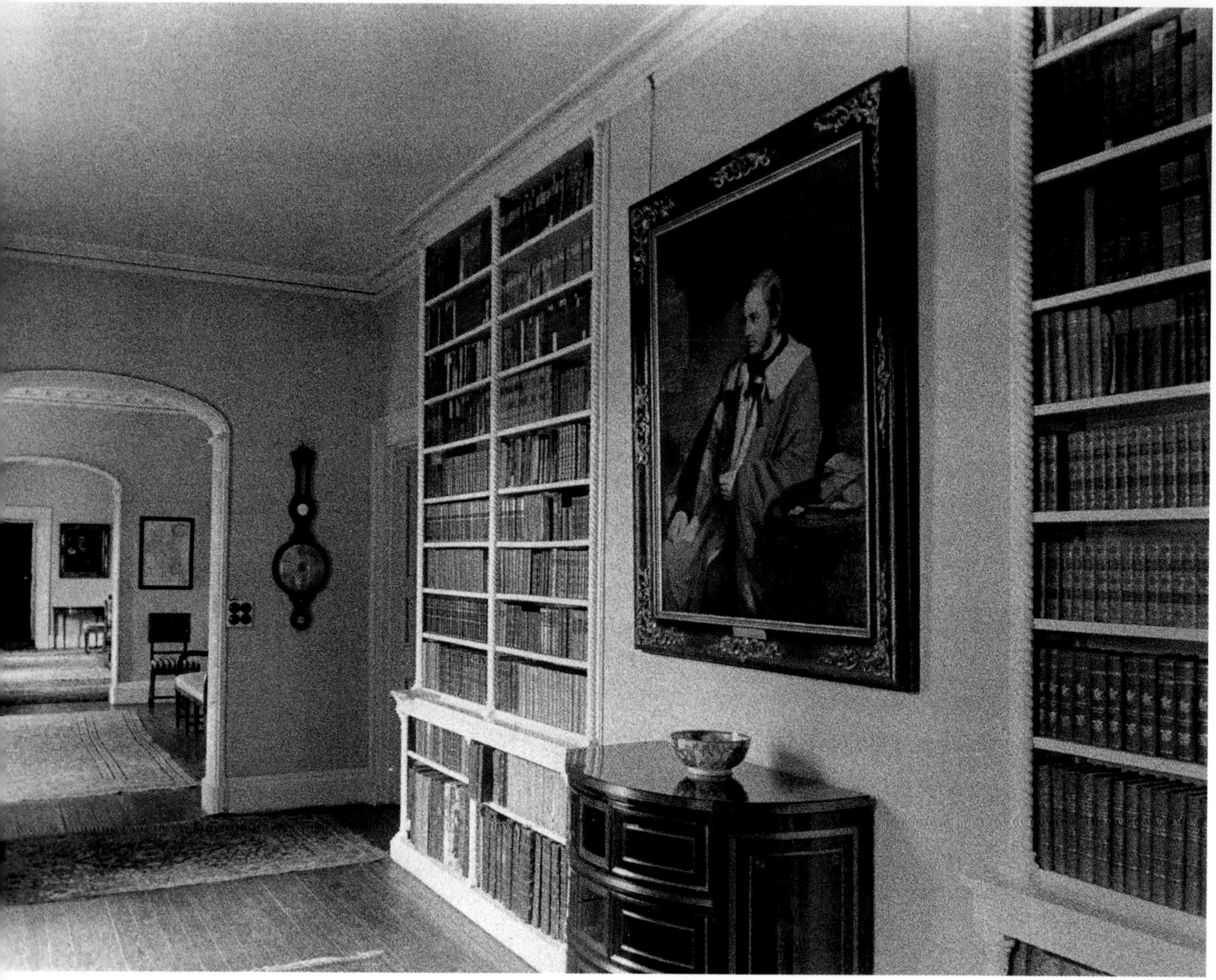

The entrance hall of Knocklofty House, looking east (1948).

Opposite page: Knocklofty House: the Box Garden (1948).

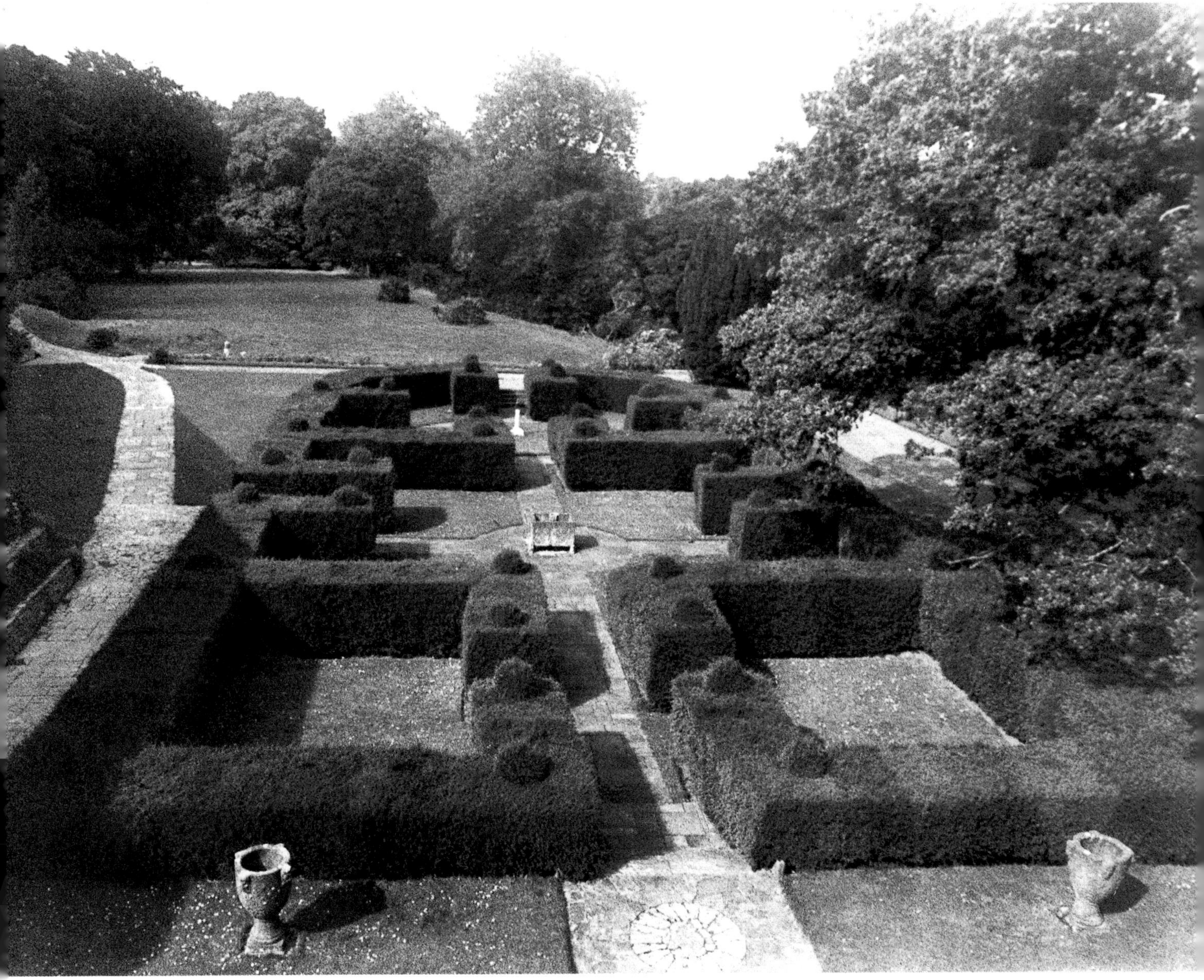

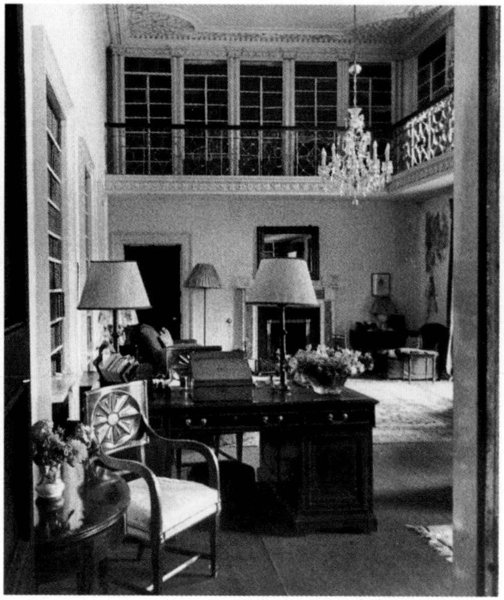

Left: Knocklofty House (1948). The two-storey library was established by Dr Hely-Hutchinson, Provost of Trinity College Dublin.

Below: Knocklofty House, showing its wonderful setting above the River Suir (1948).

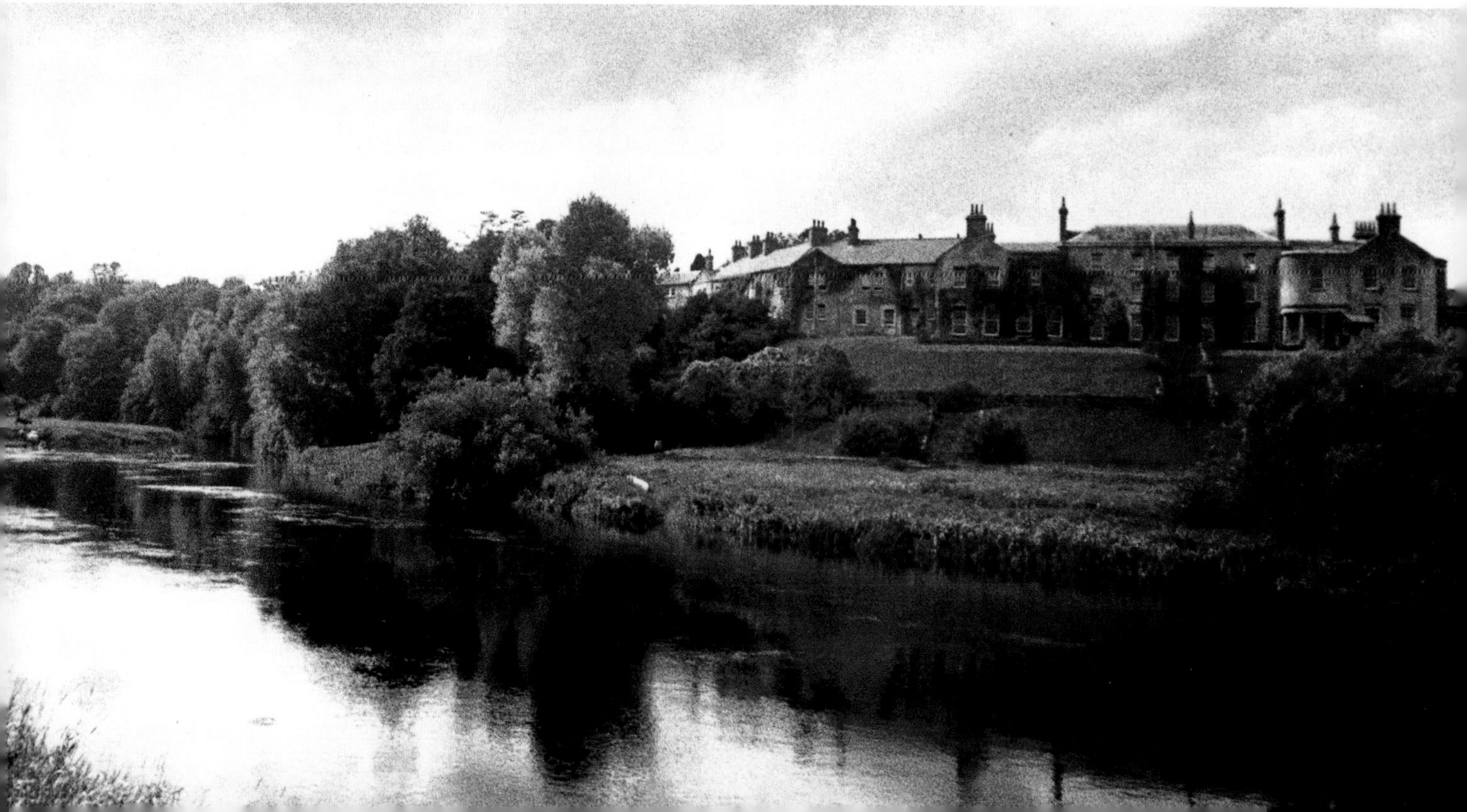

Fair Days

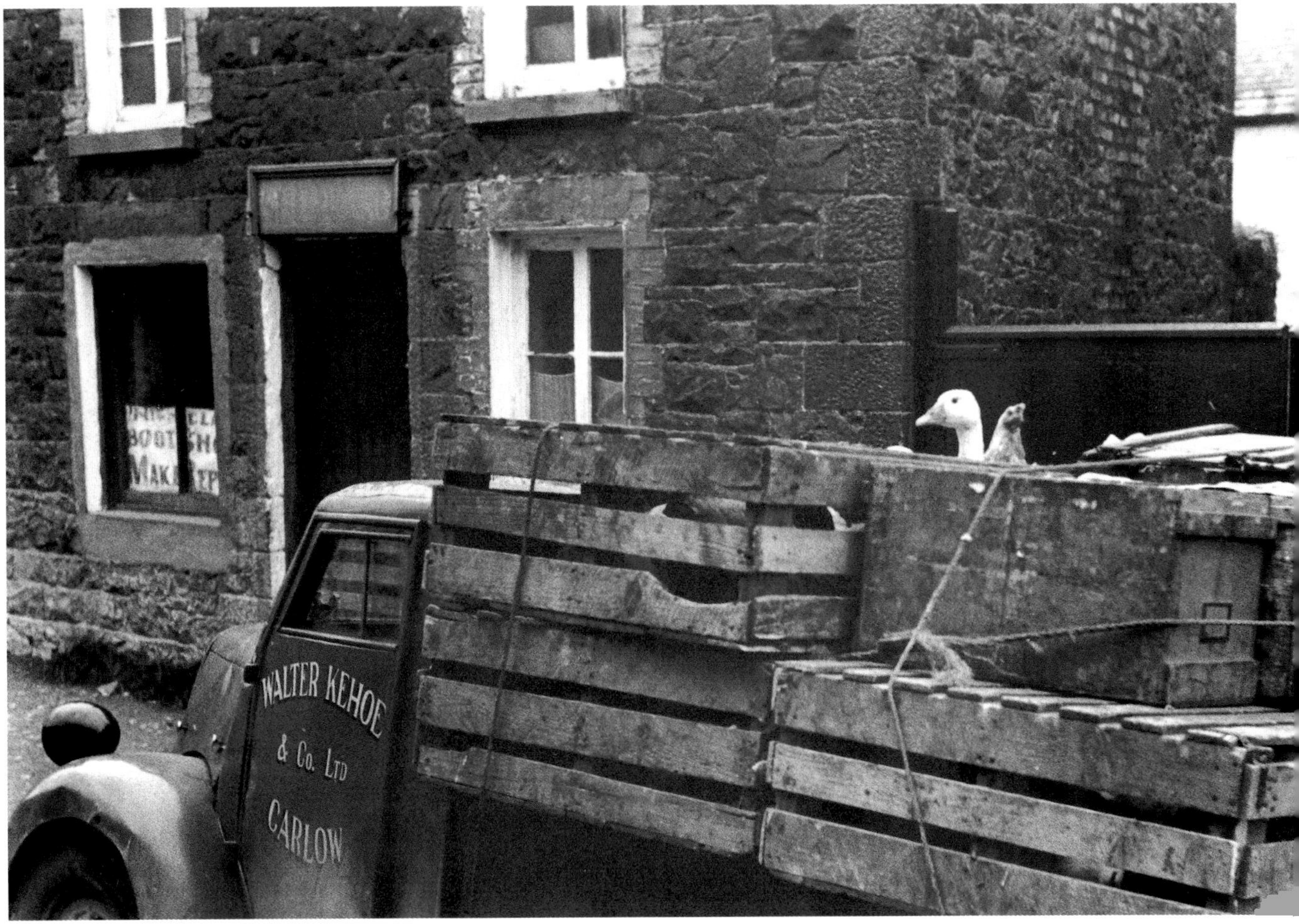

Fair Day, Clonmel (1947): 'Goosey, Goosey, Gander!'

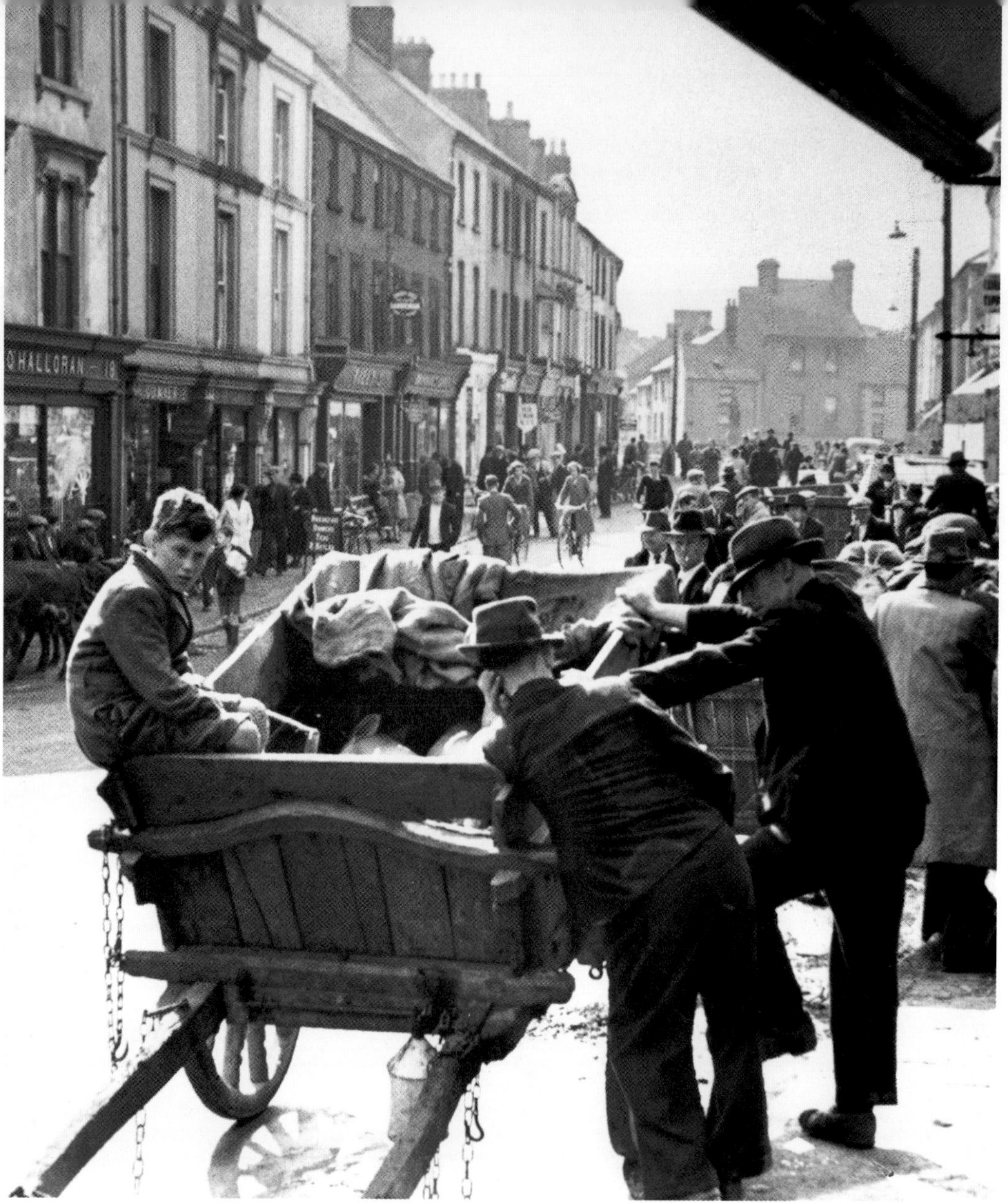

Fair Day, Tipperary town (1940).

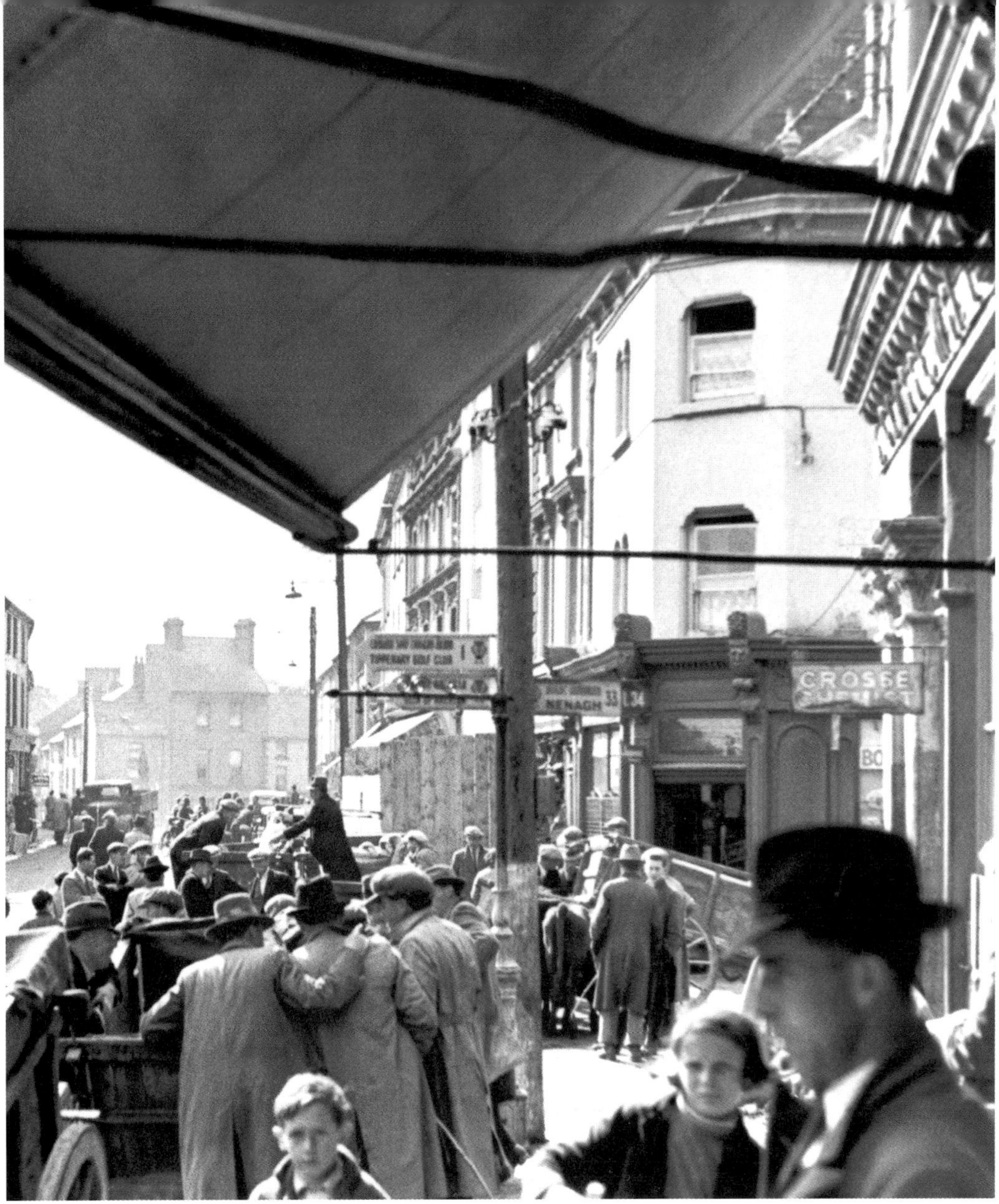

Fair Day, Tipperary town (1940).

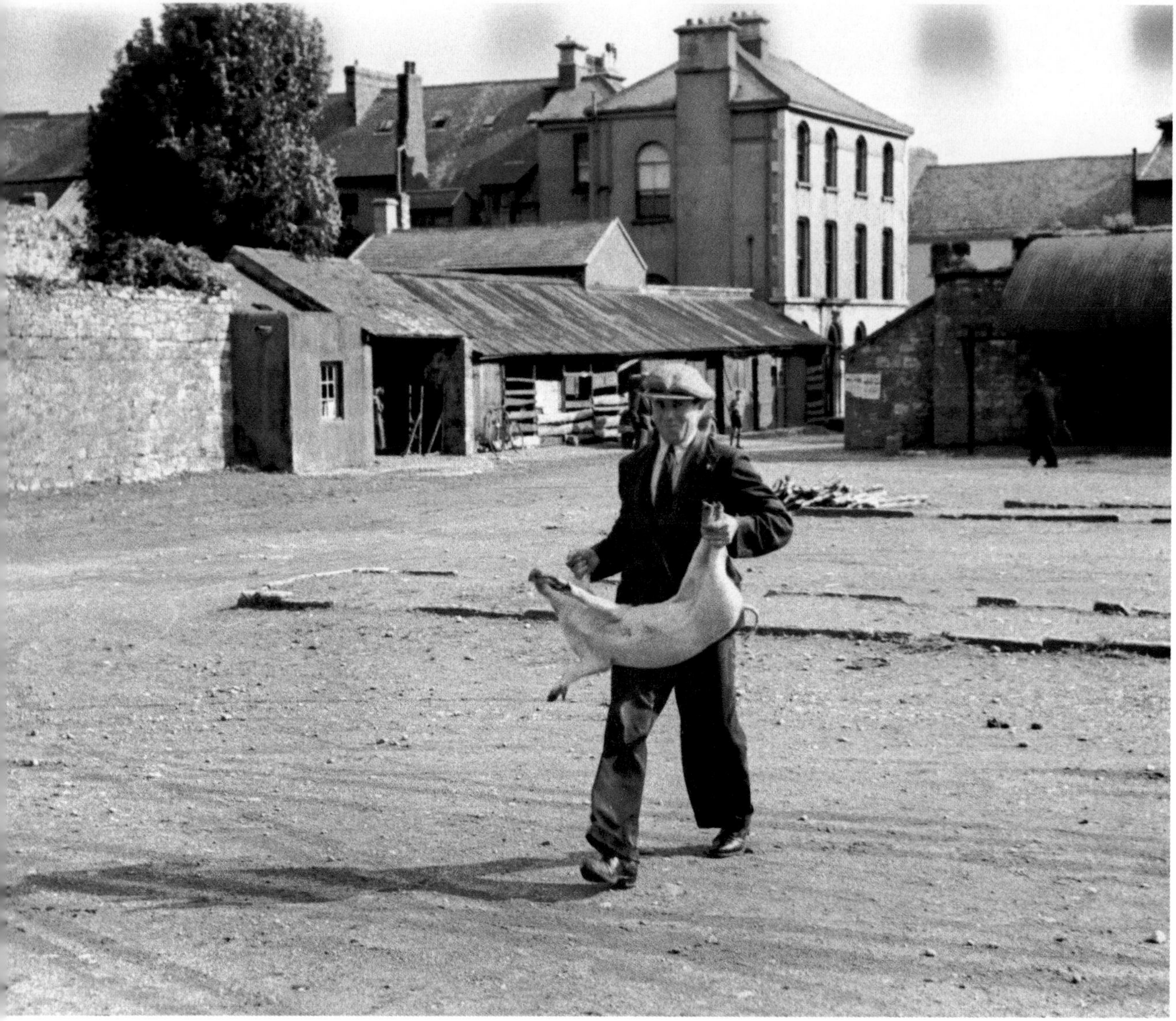

Above and opposite page: Fair Day, Tipperary town (1940).

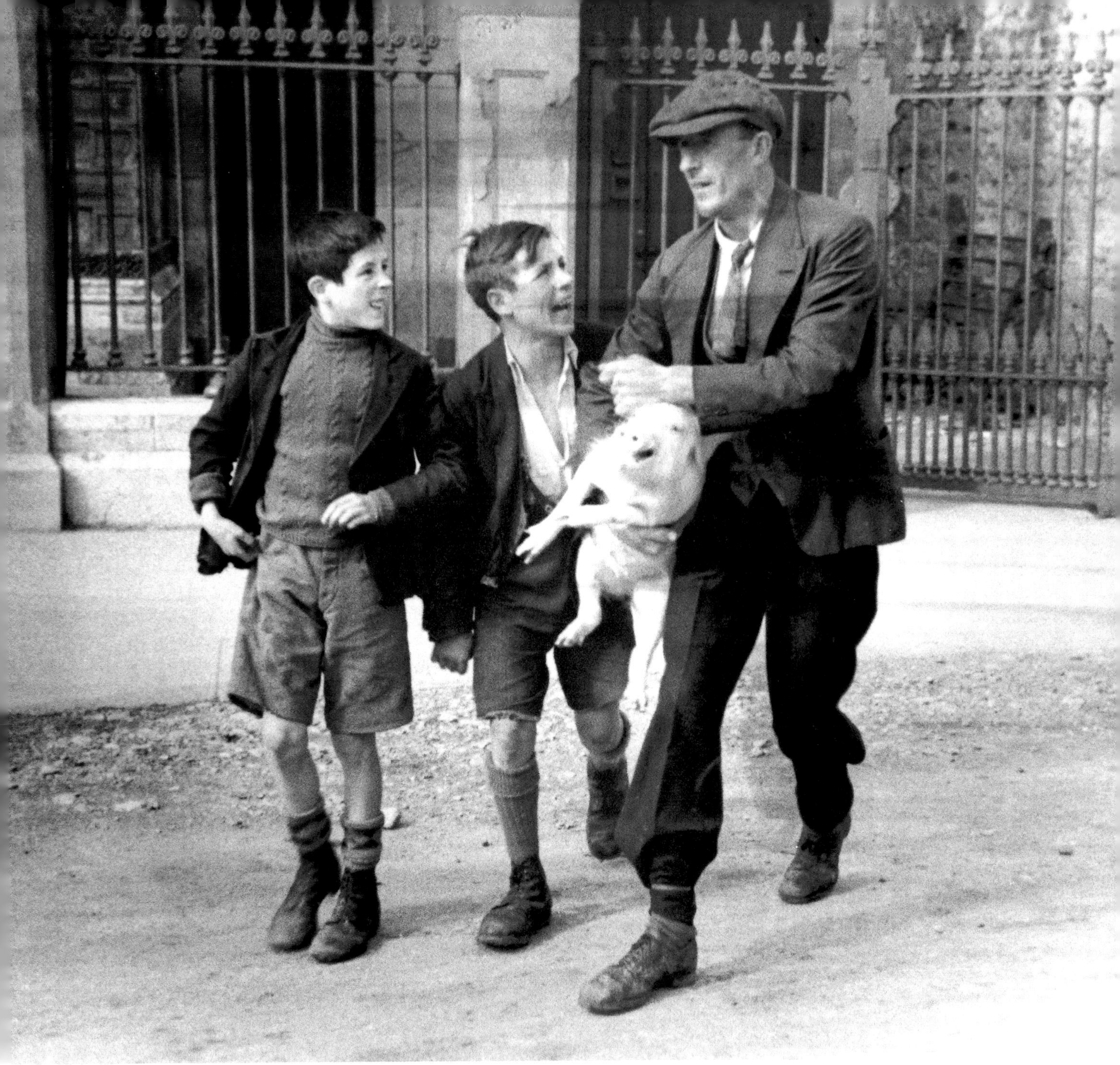

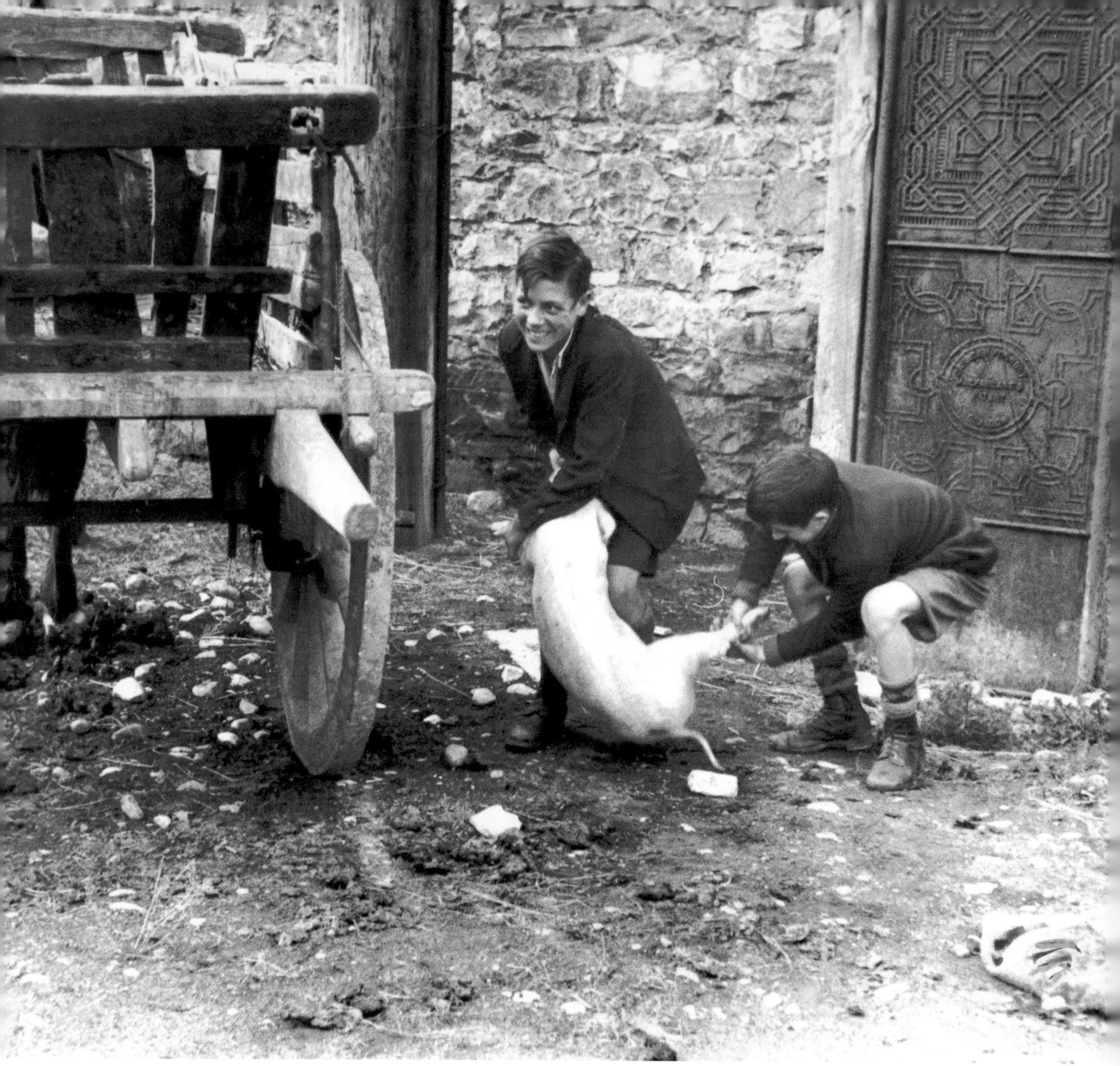

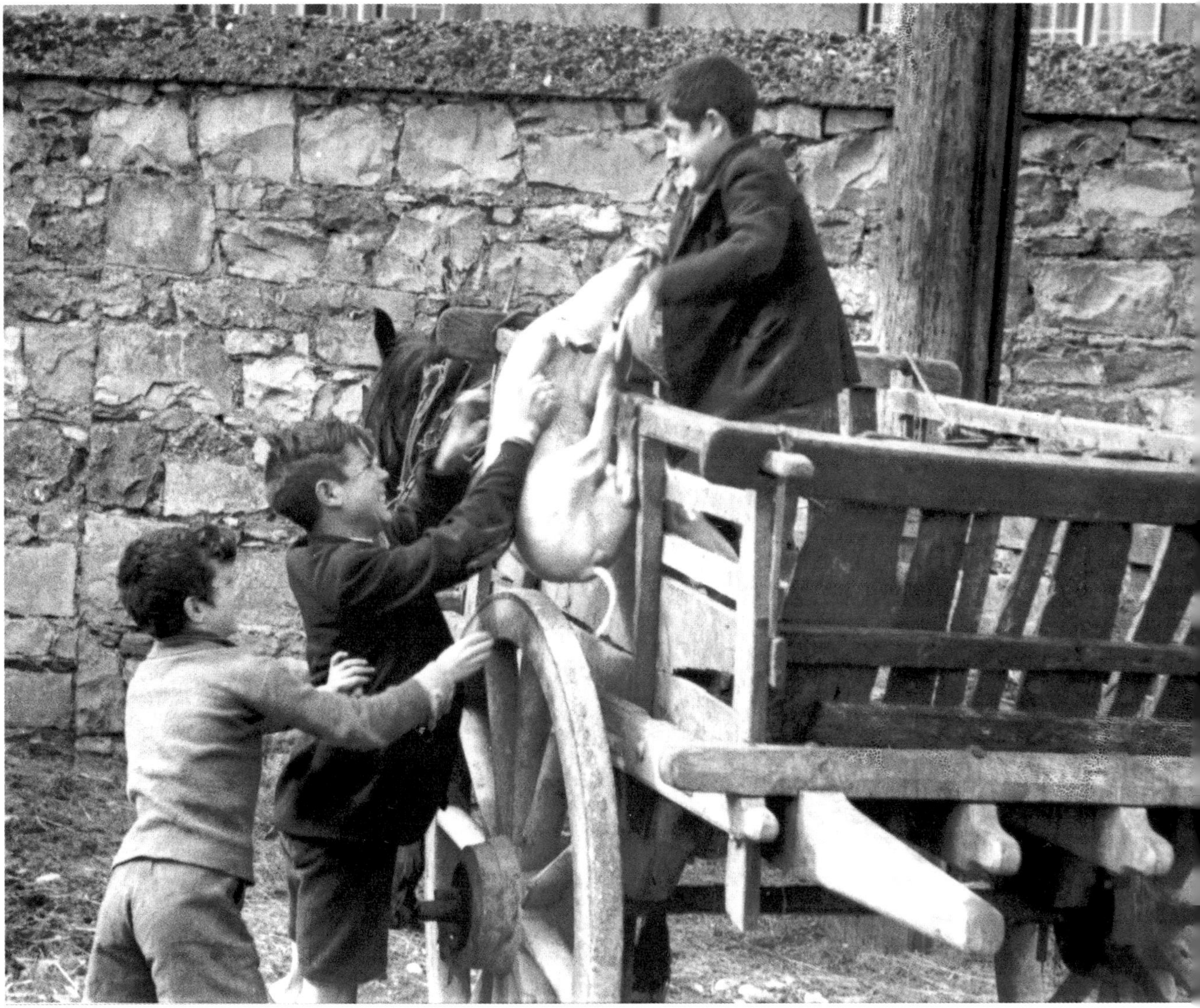

Above and opposite page: Fair Day, Tipperary town (1940).

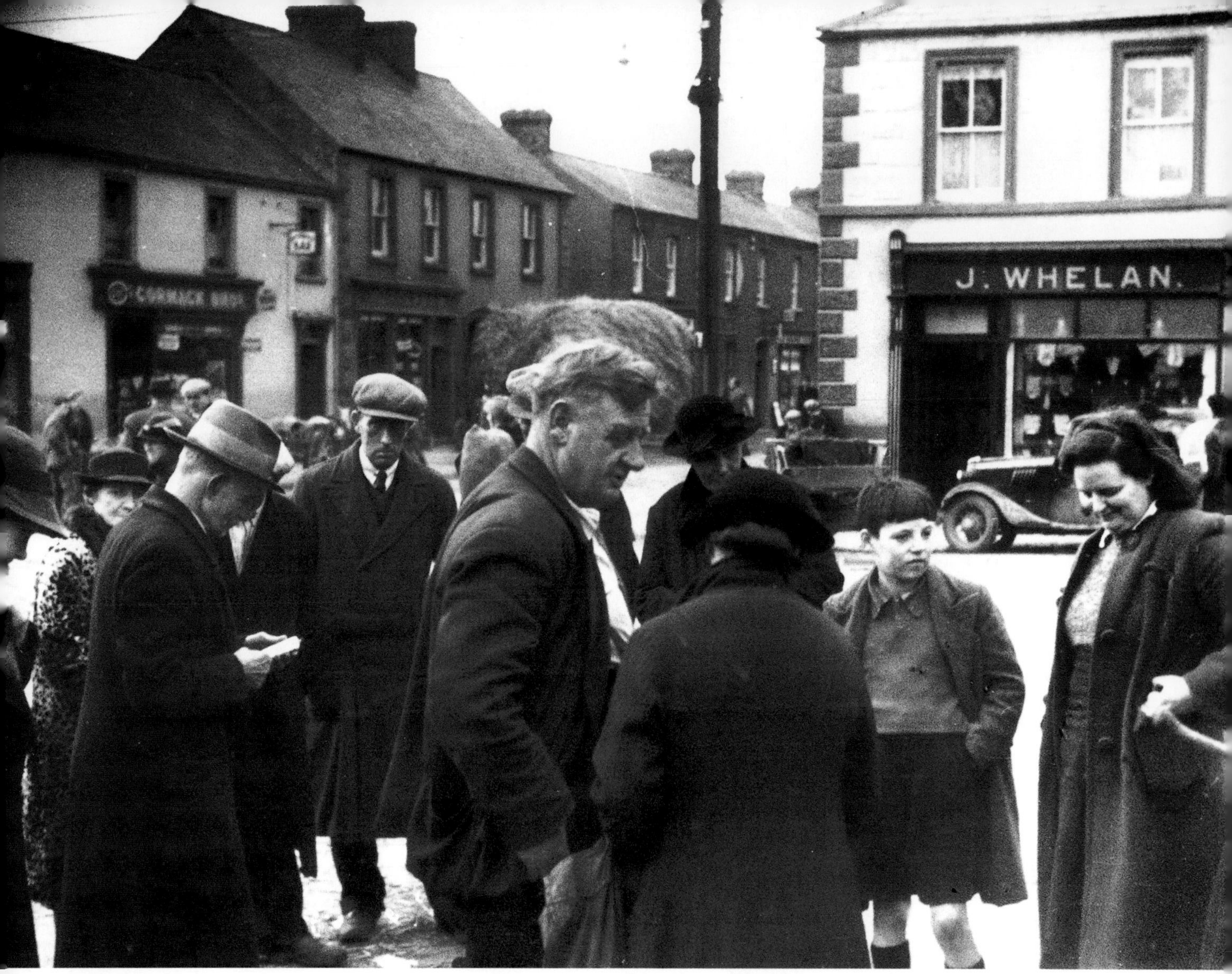

Fair Day, Cashel (1942).

At Work

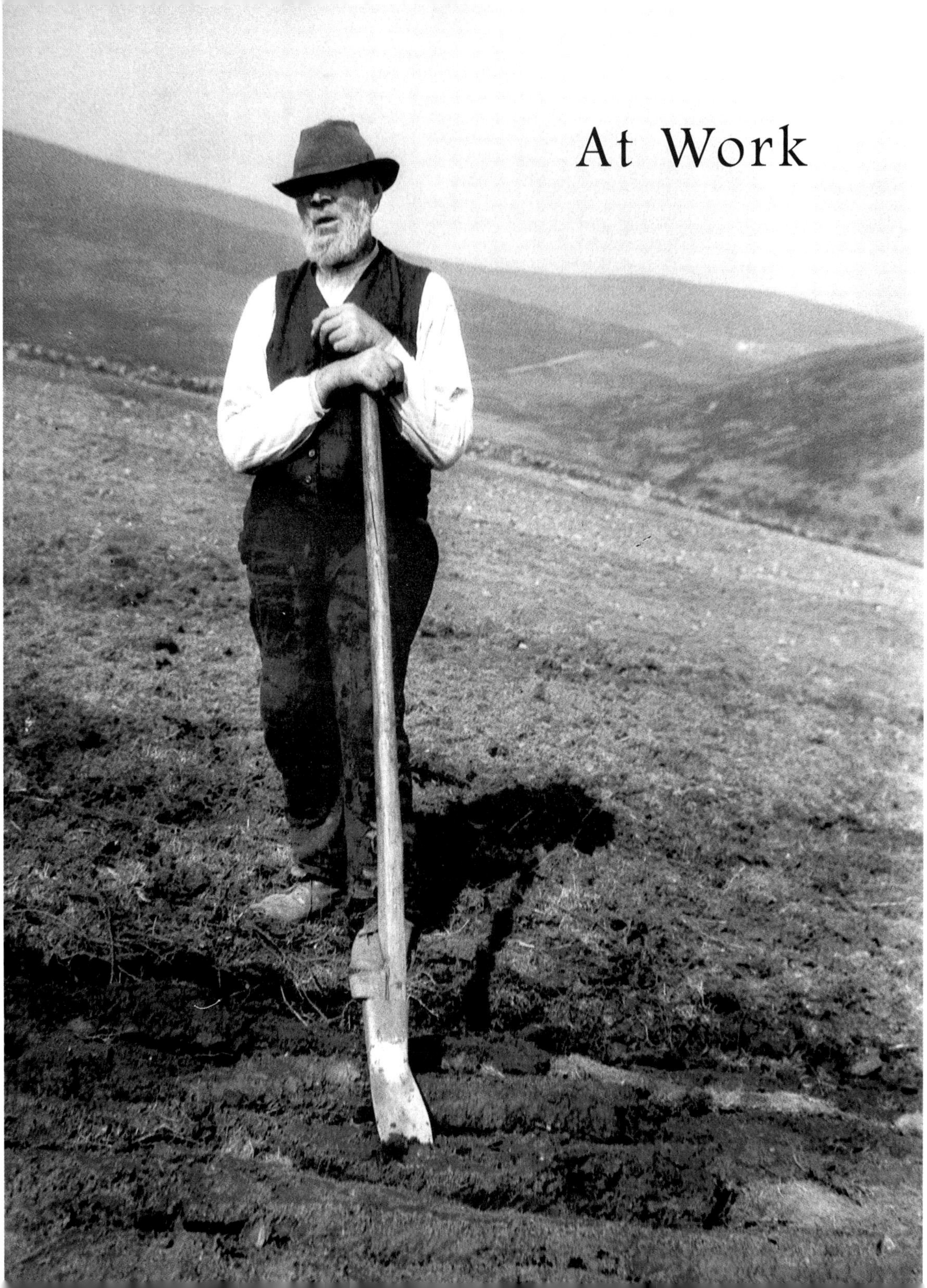

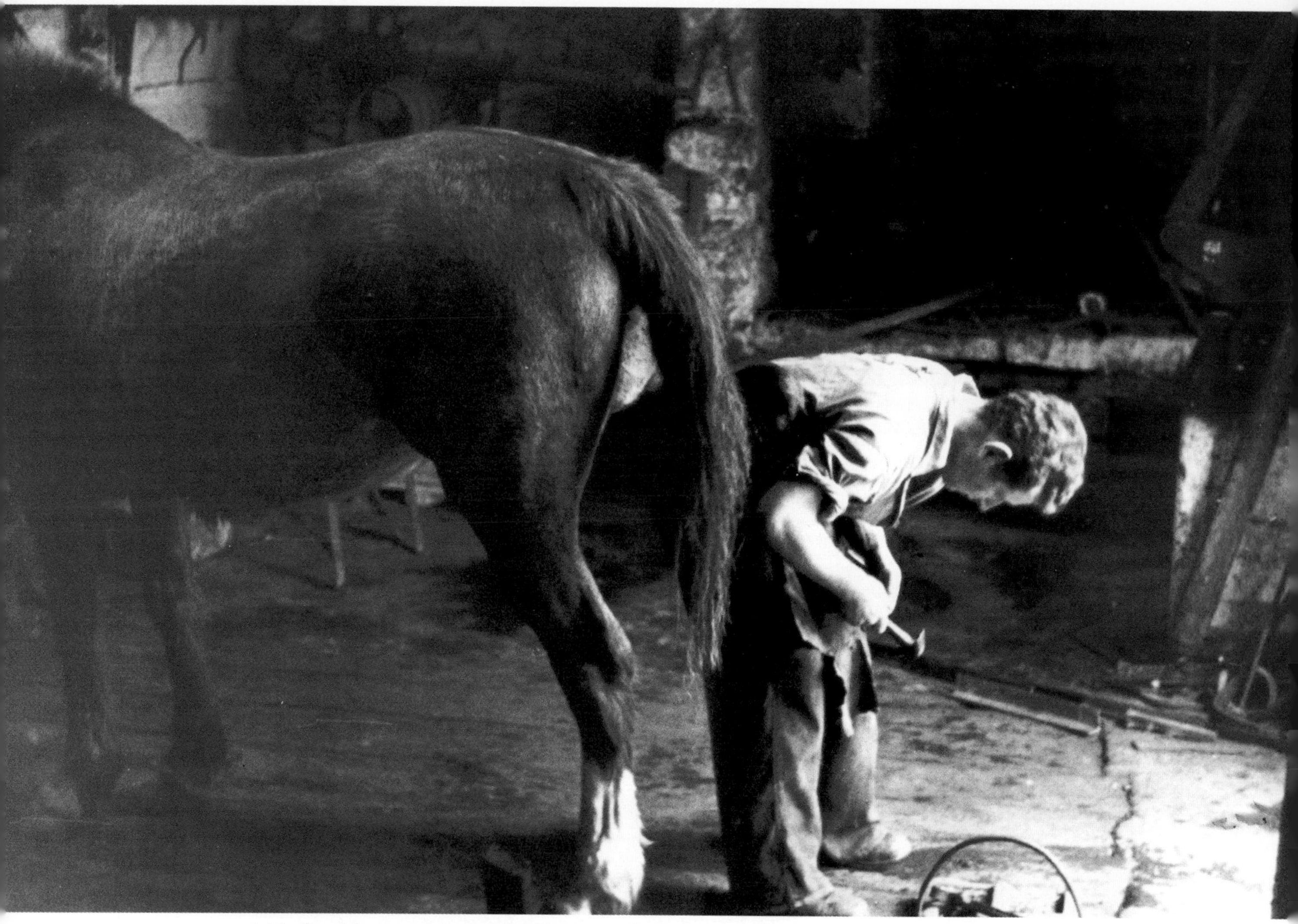

A blacksmith at work in the old forge at Ballypatrick (1944).

Previous page: Turf-cutting in the foothills of the Knockmealdown Mountains. The long-bladed spade, the slean, is peculiar to Ireland and varies somewhat from county to county (1929).

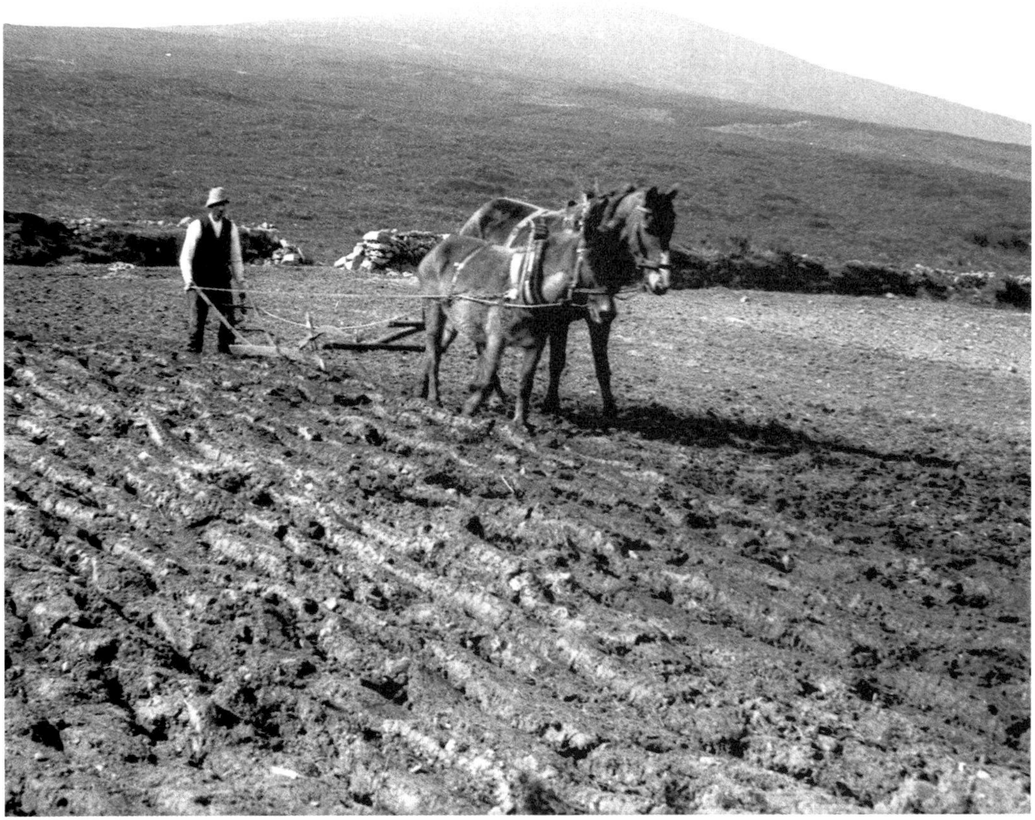

Ploughing in the Knockmealdown Mountains, the old way (1929).

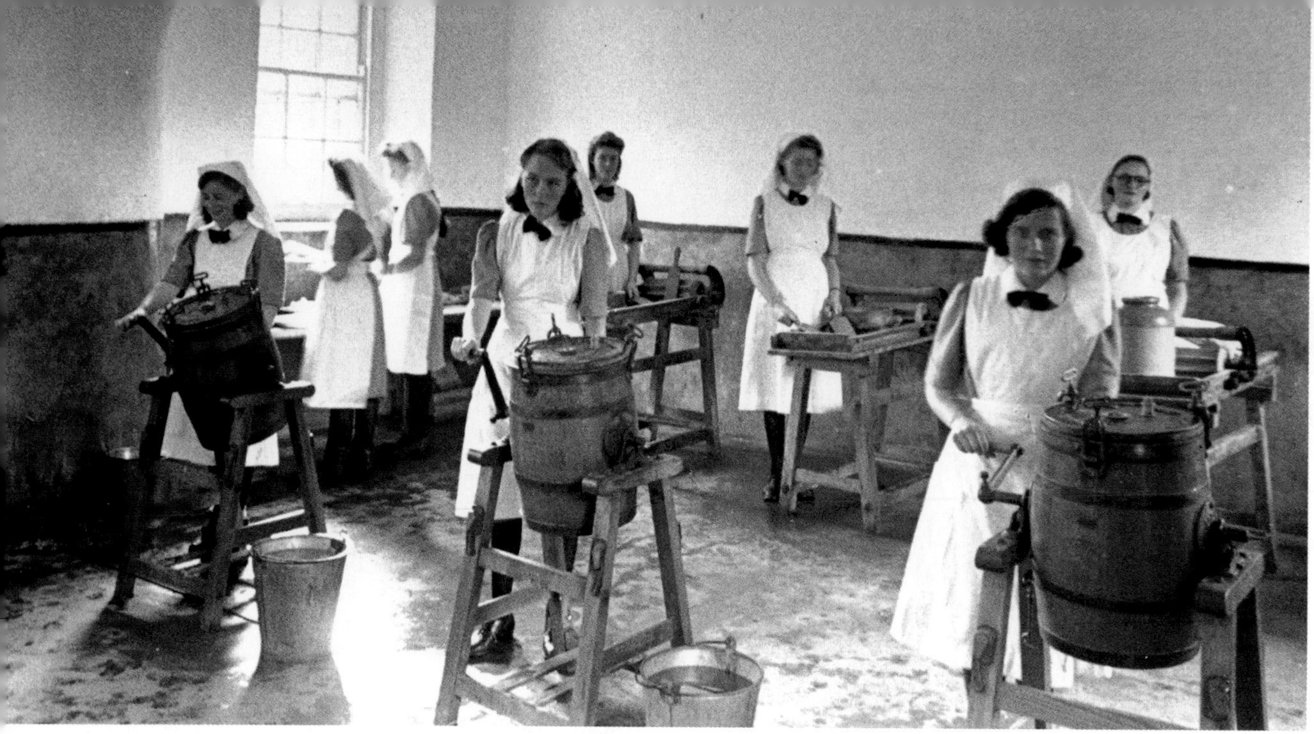

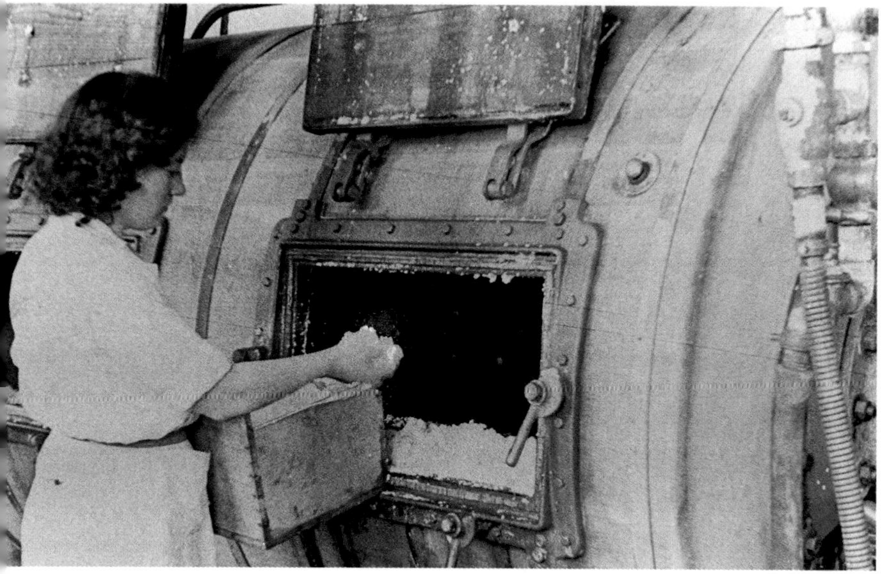

Above: Butter-making class at the College of Domestic Science, Dundrum (1944). The college, which had over forty students, was run by the Presentation Sisters.

Left: Butter-making on a larger scale at the creamery in Ballypatrick (1944). This old creamery is still standing but is surrounded by the much larger premises of Glanbia Ltd. The Ballypatrick Co-operative Dairy Society was founded in 1893.

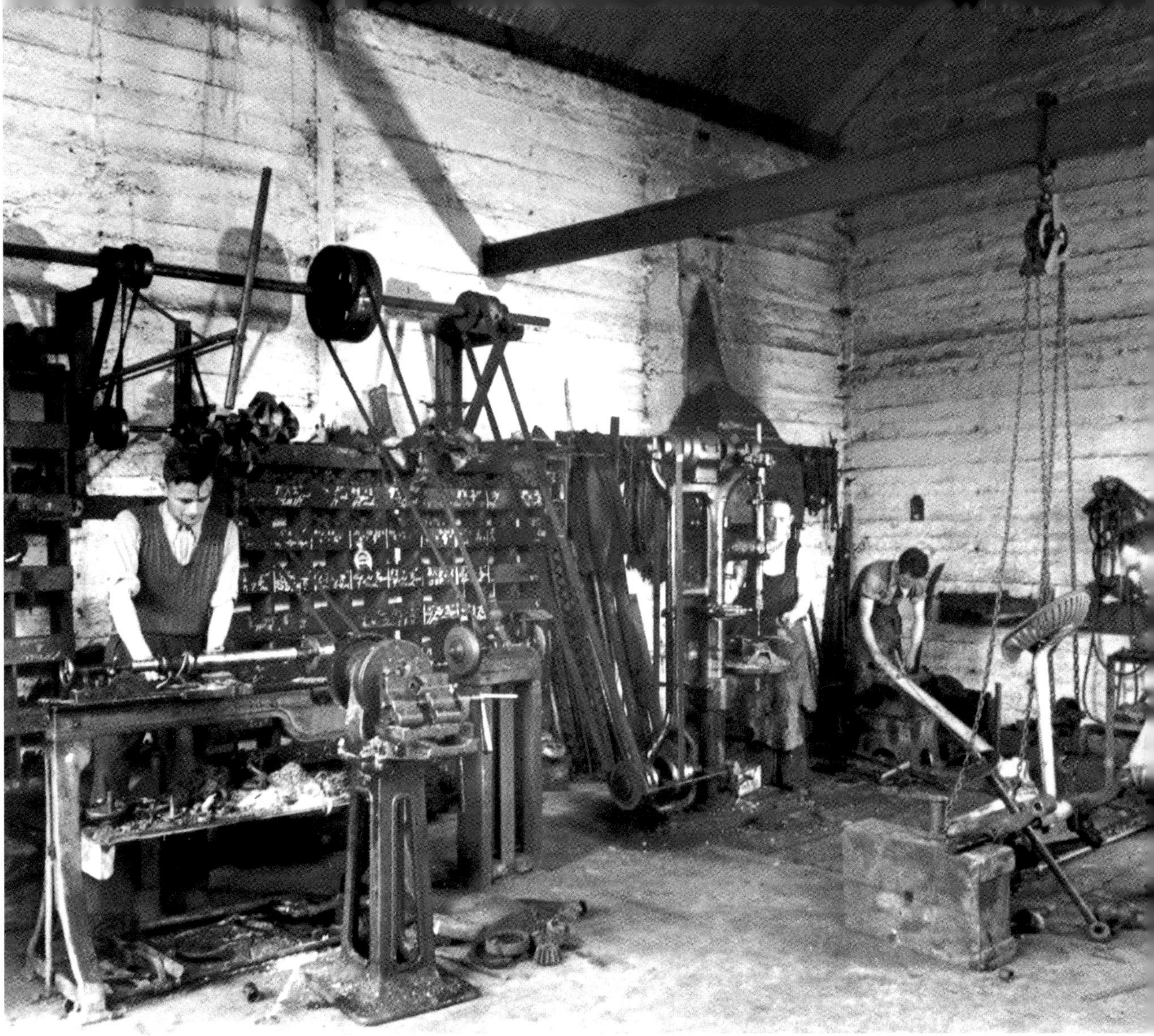

Inside Gibbs' Engineering Works, Ballypatrick (1944). The firm is still in business. Michael Gibbs has taken over from his father, Bill, and the establishment has moved to a much larger site.

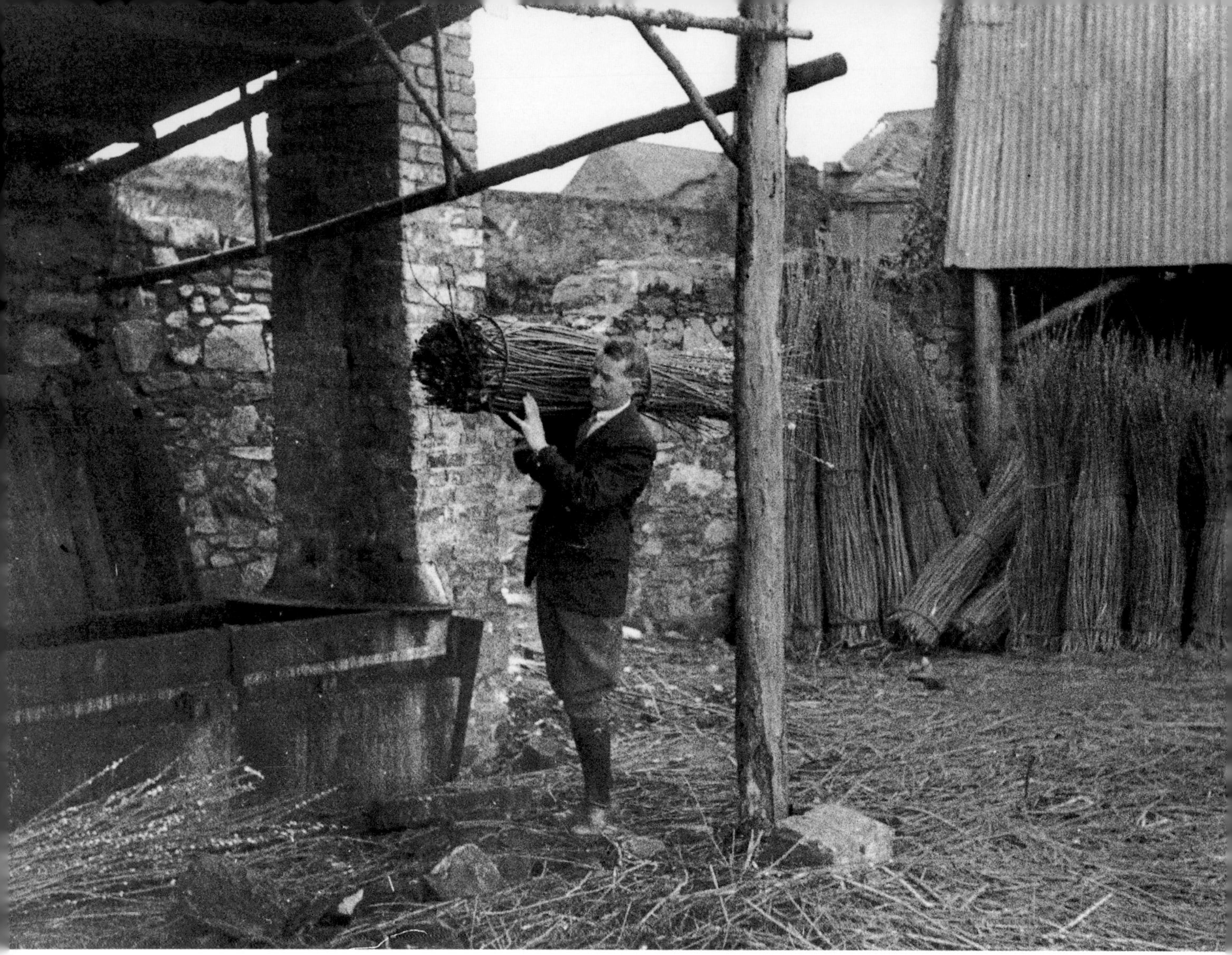

Carrick Furniture (1936). Once they have been de-barked in the factory yard, the sallies are brought indoors for moulding.

Opposite page: Demolishing an old house on Main Street, Carrick-on-Suir (1936).

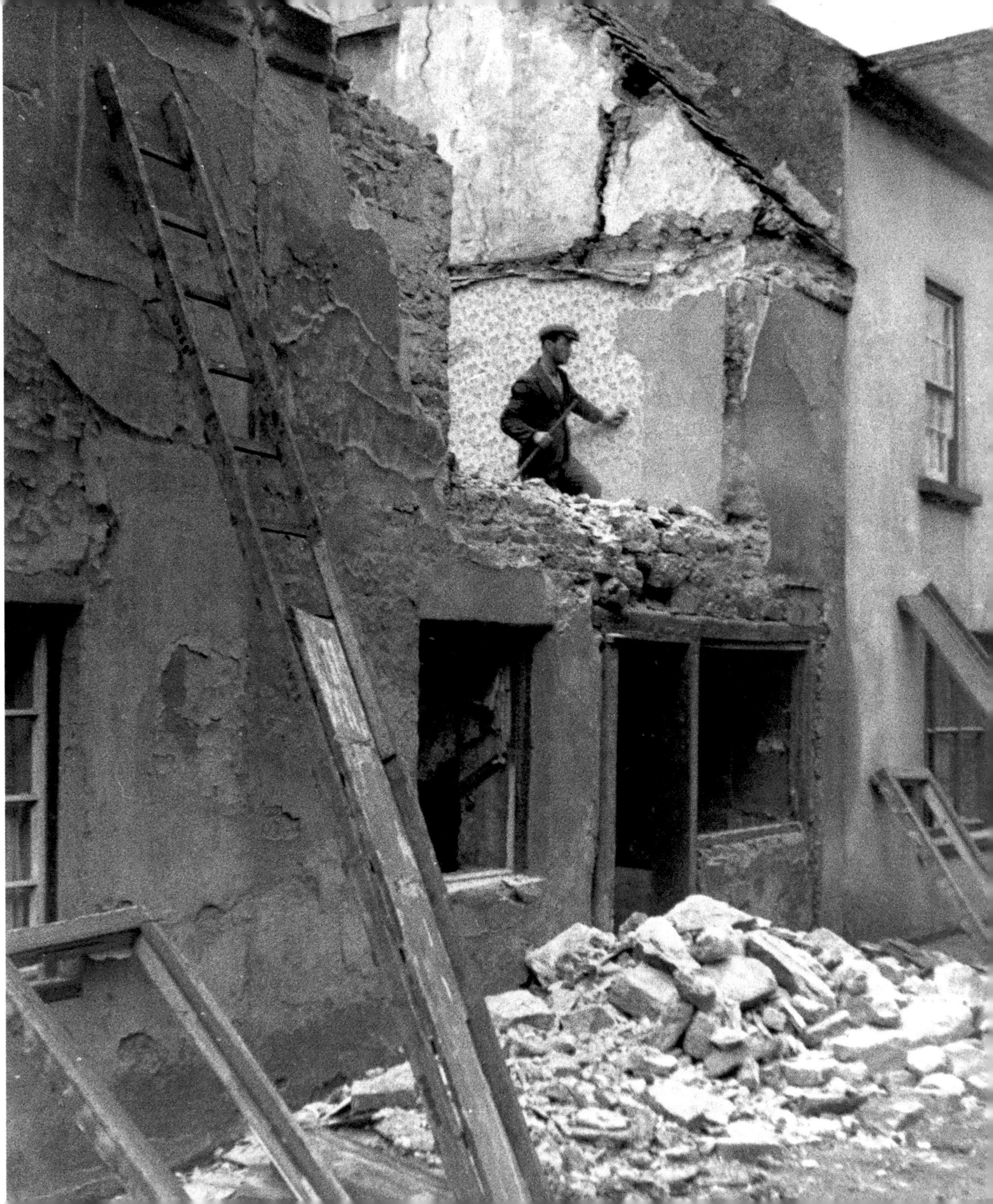

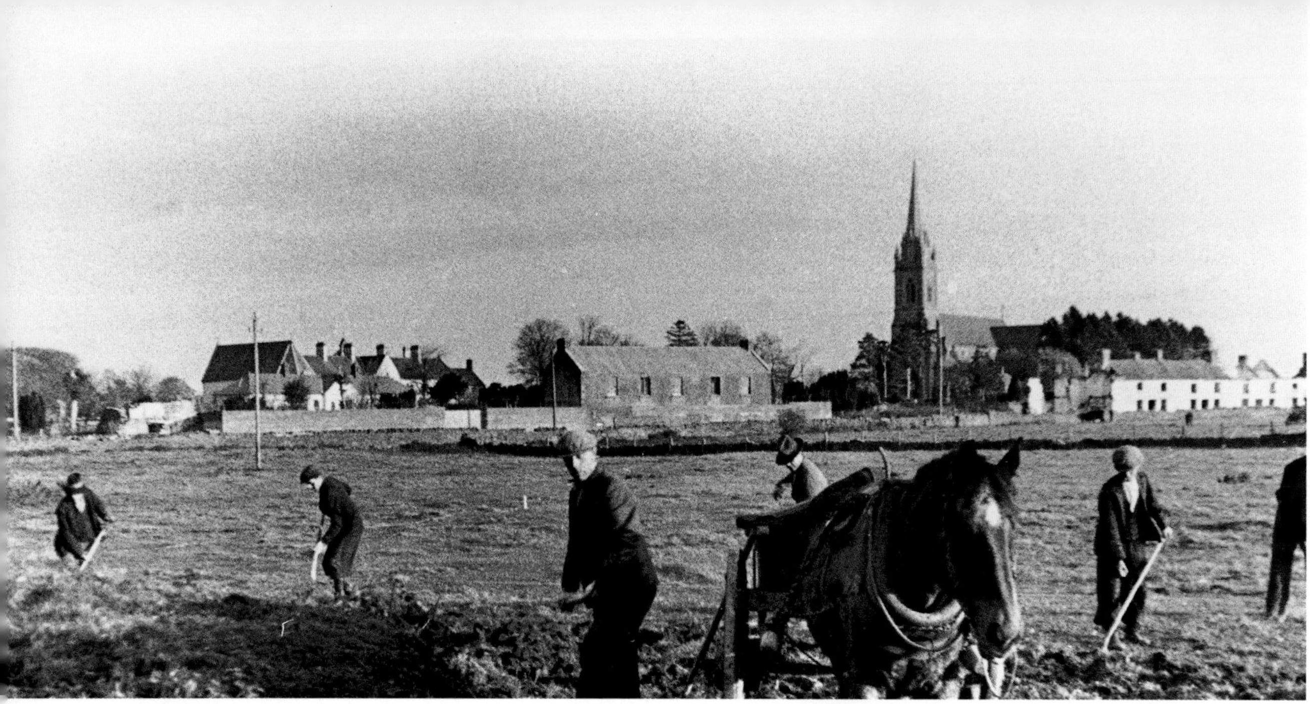

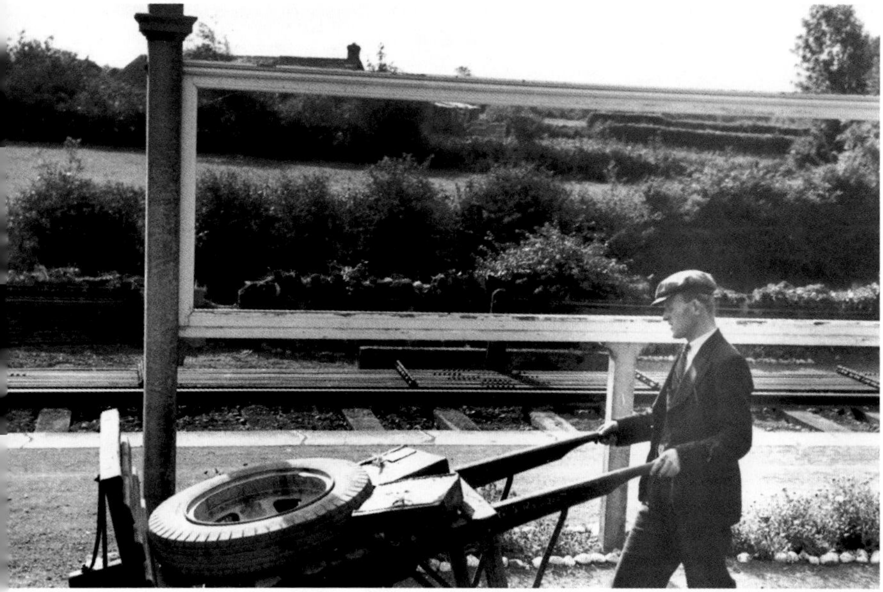

Above: Workmen digging the foundations for a new factory in Templemore (1937). The finished factory was that of Lancegaye Safety Glass (Ireland) Ltd.

Left: A porter at Limerick Junction (1940). Note that the name-board has been removed: this was to confuse enemy paratroops who might drop in unannounced during 'The Emergency'.

Scenery

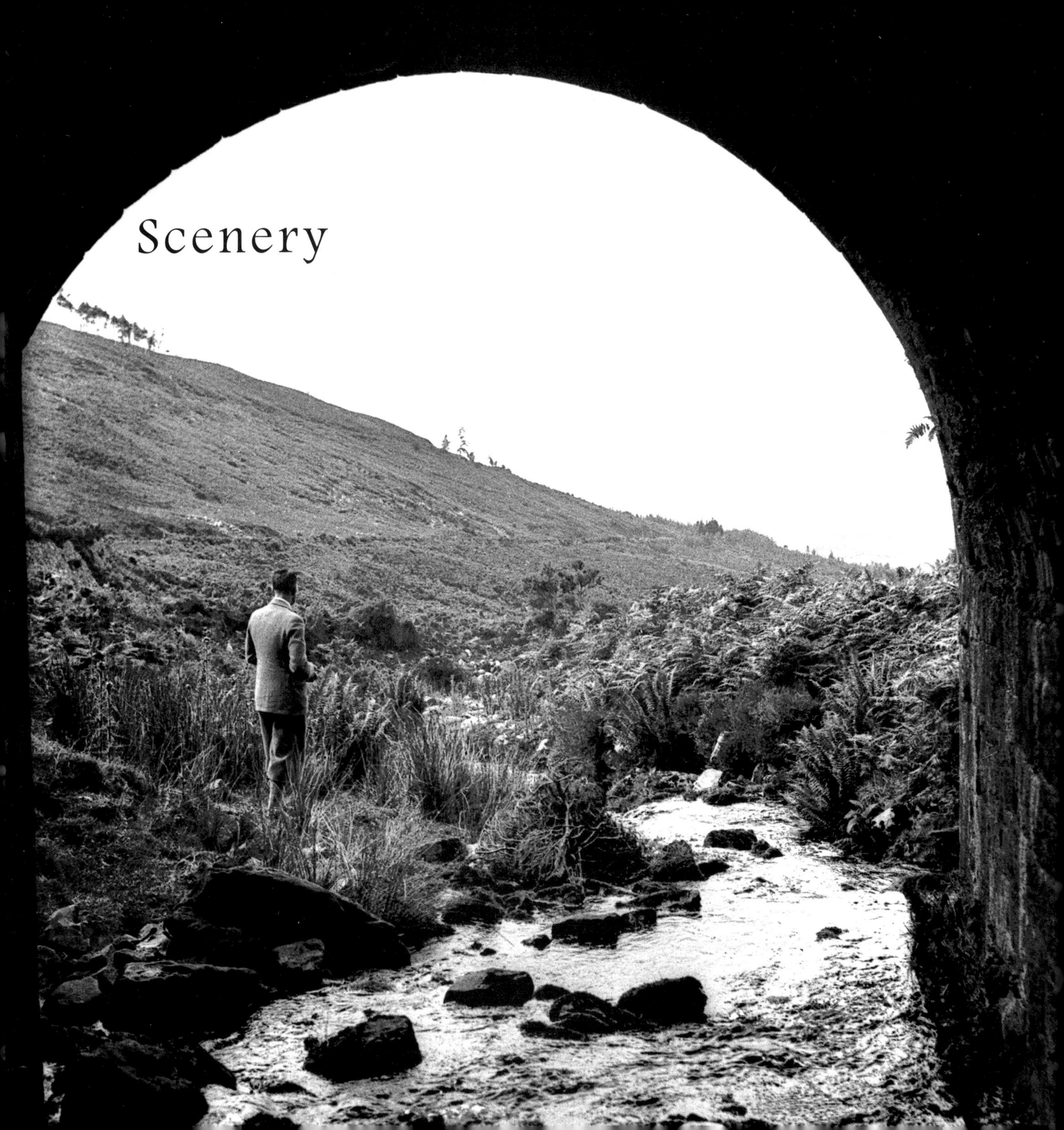

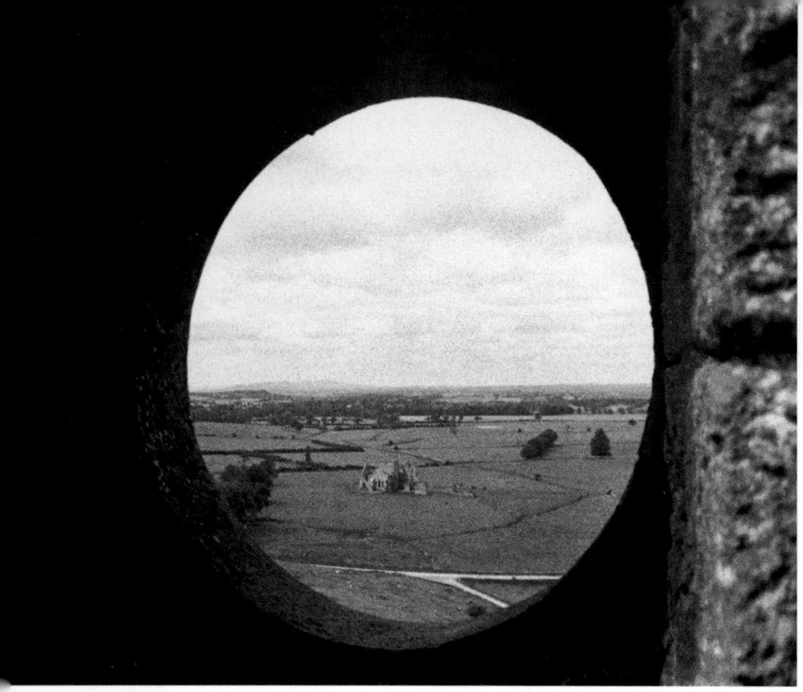

Left: View of Tipperary taken through the Round Window of the Rock of Cashel (1945).

Previous page: Under the bridge at Baylough (1931). The River Duag is a tributary of the Tar, which, in turn, is a tributary of the Suir.

Below: Dr and Mrs Bourke of Melbourne, Australia, with Father Browne and their chauffeur, pose with three 'locals' in the Knockmealdown Mountains (1926).

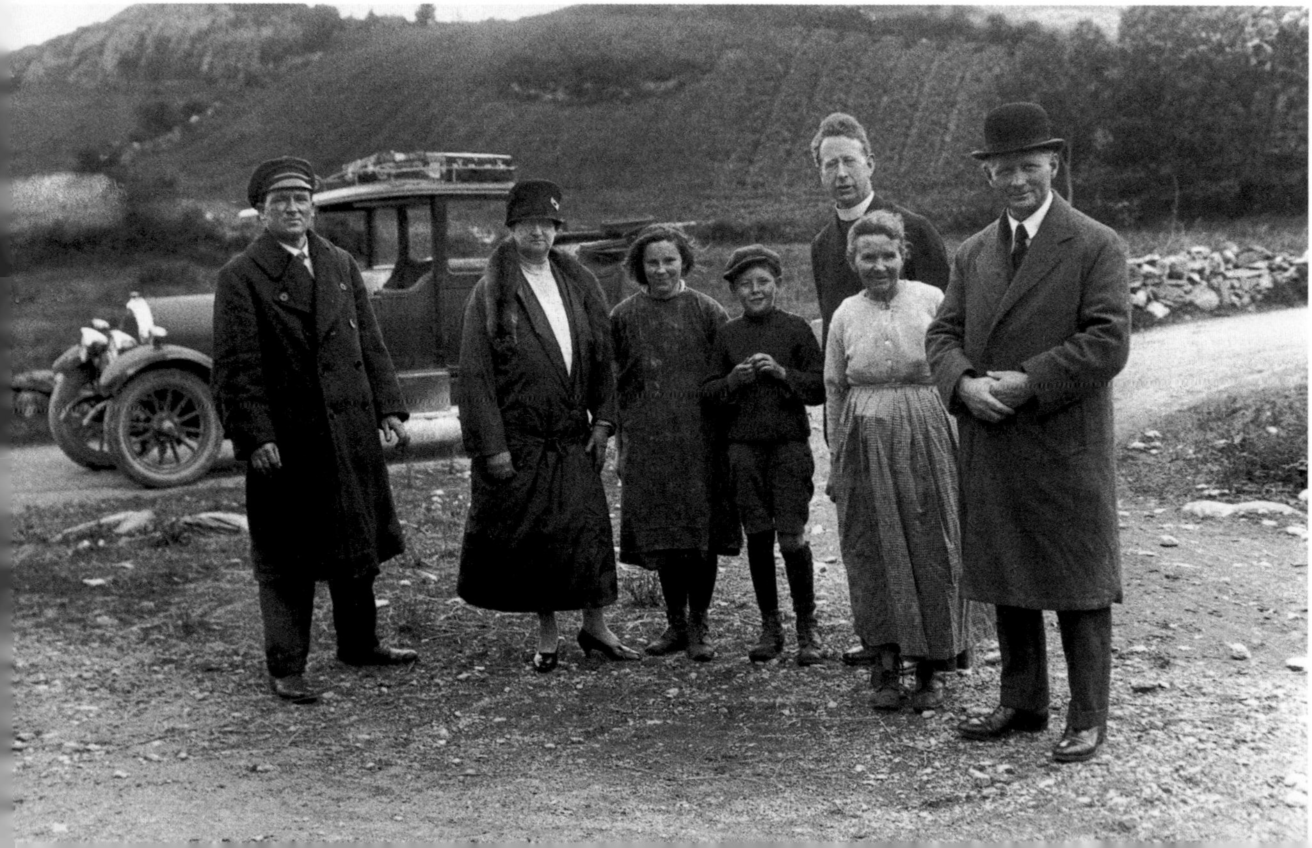

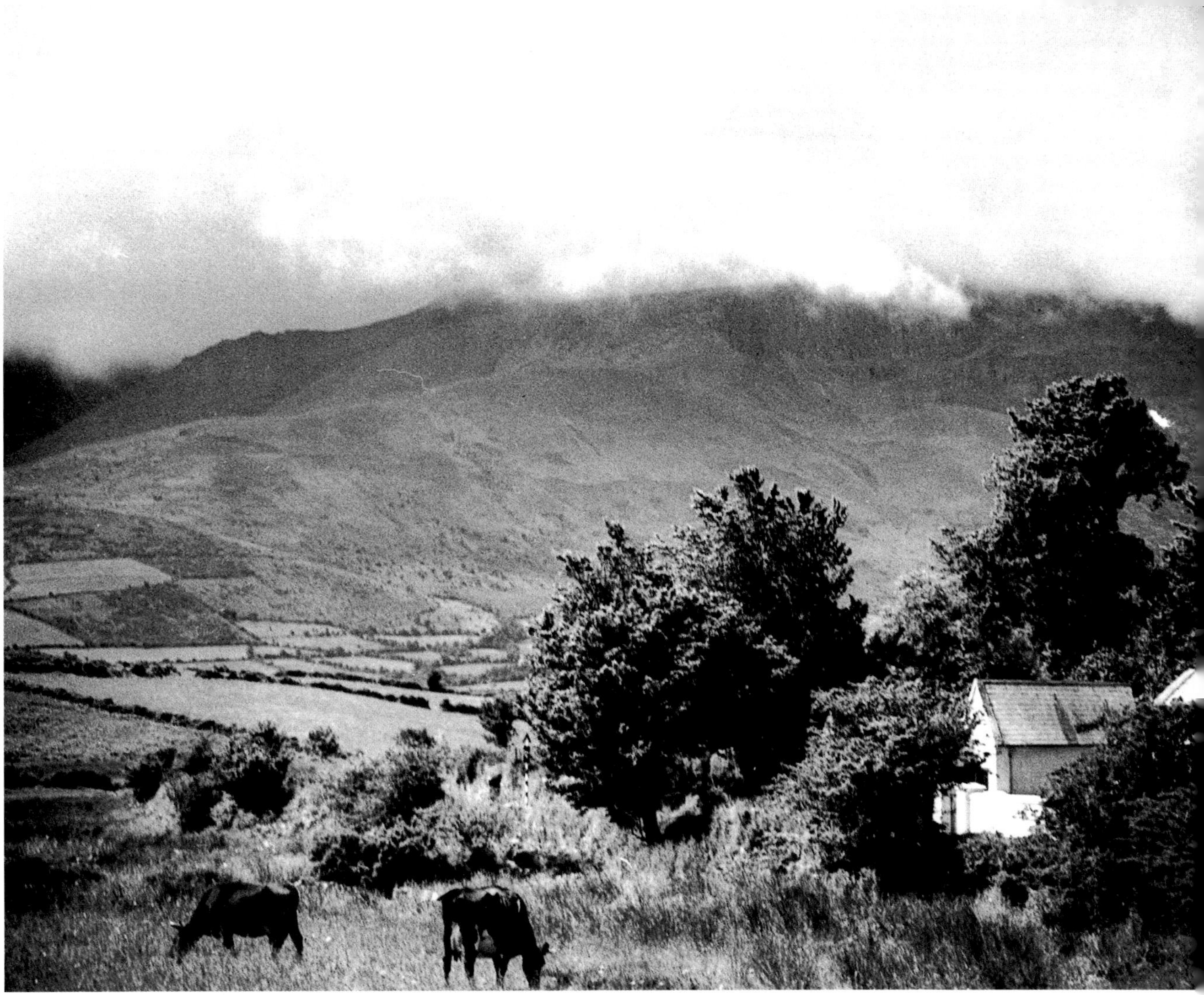

Pastoral scene in the Galtee Mountains near Coolboy (1931). Father Browne went on to climb Galtymore mountain, 919 metres.

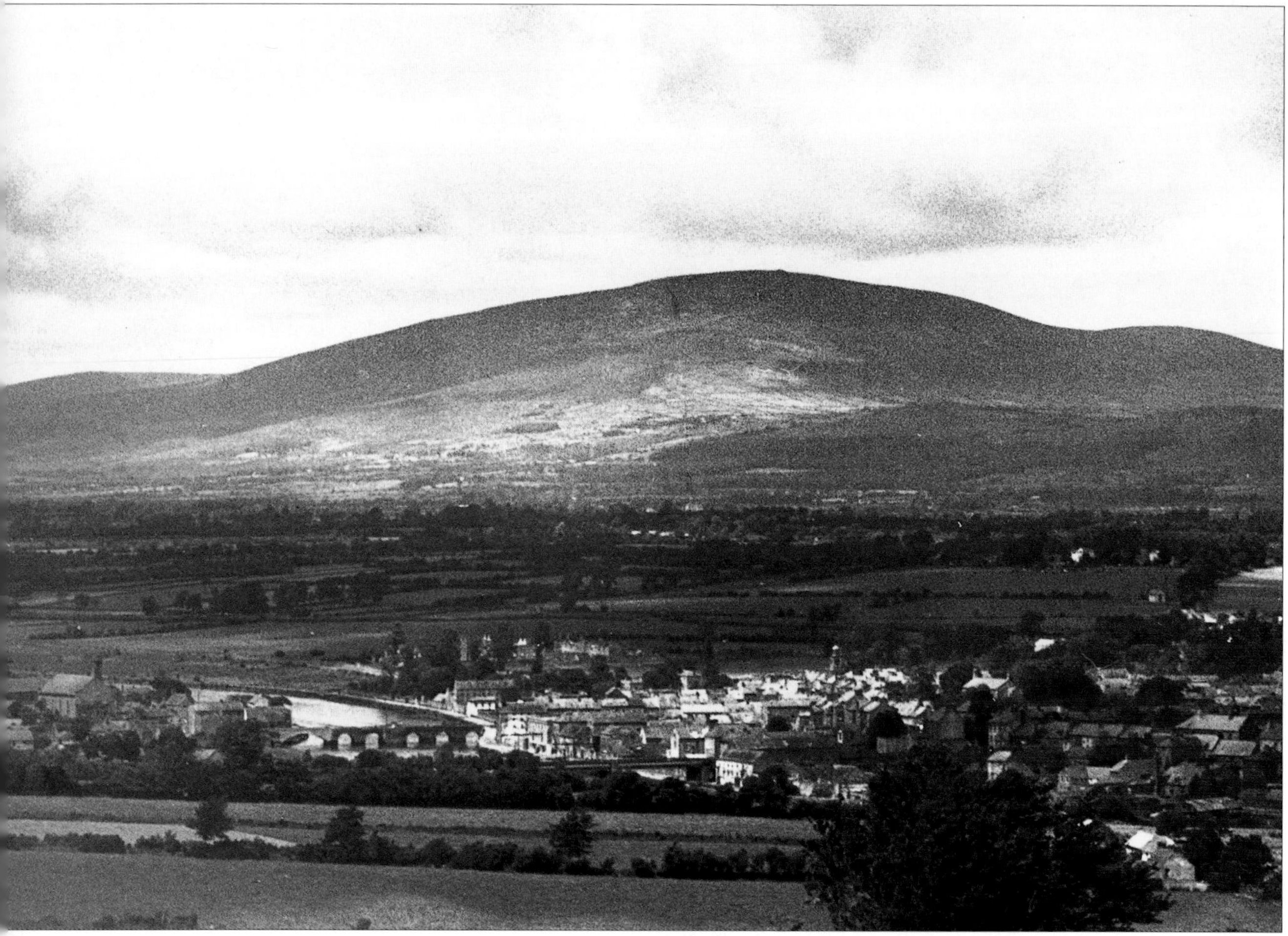

Carrick-on-Suir and Slievenamon, taken from 'The Devil's Elbow' on the Dungarvan Road (1931).

Opposite page: A view of Carrick-on-Suir from a distance, basking under an isolated puffy white cloud (1936).

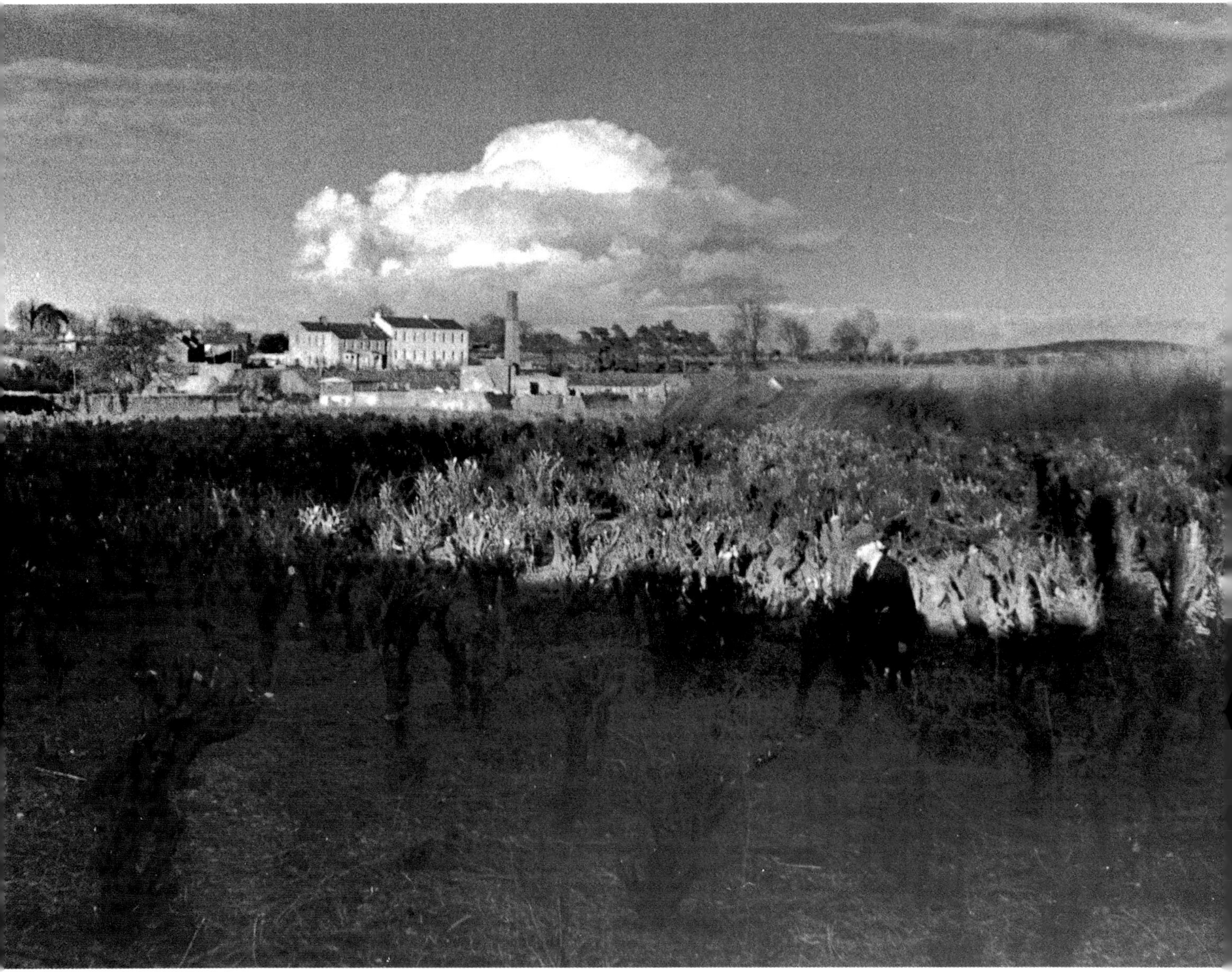

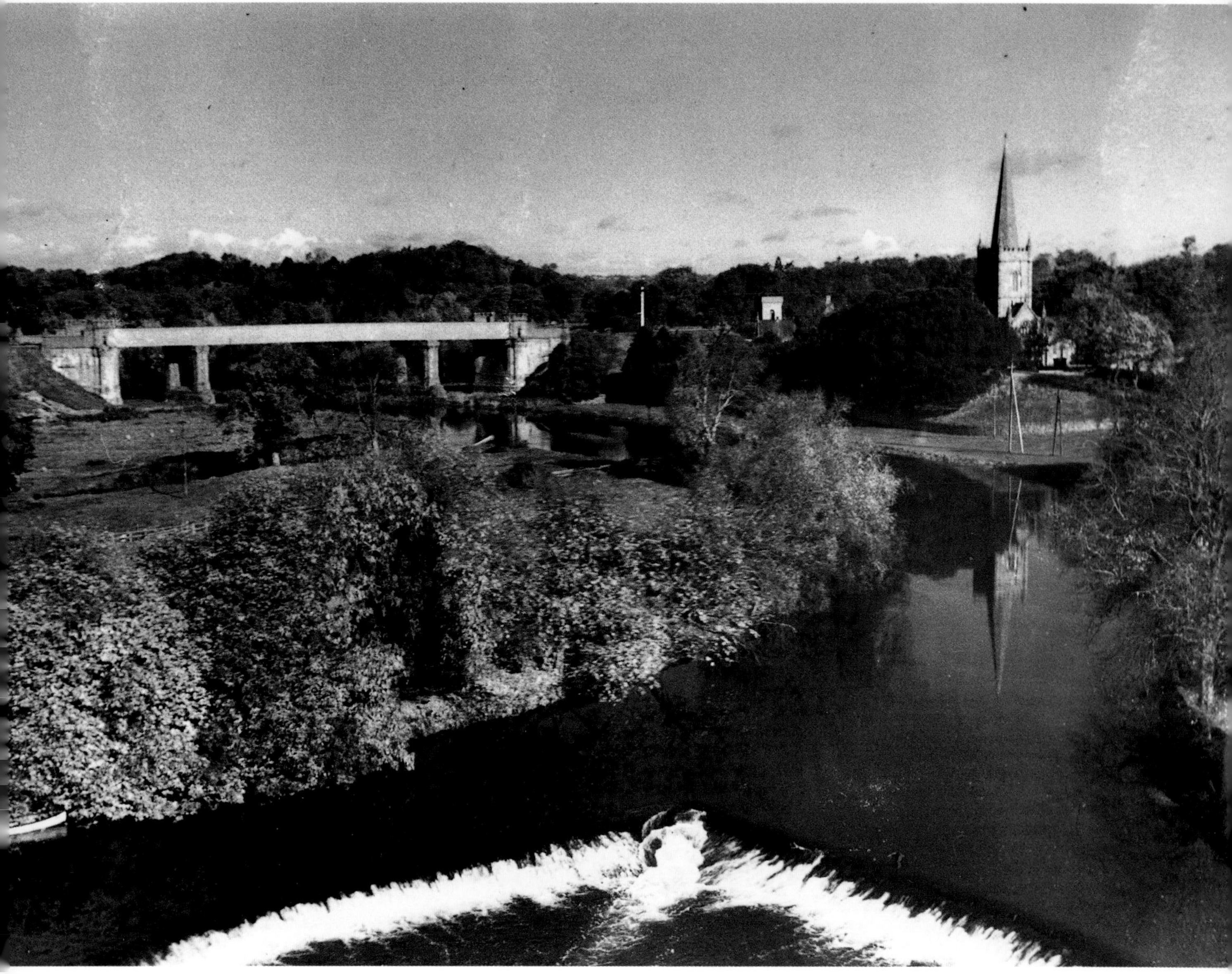

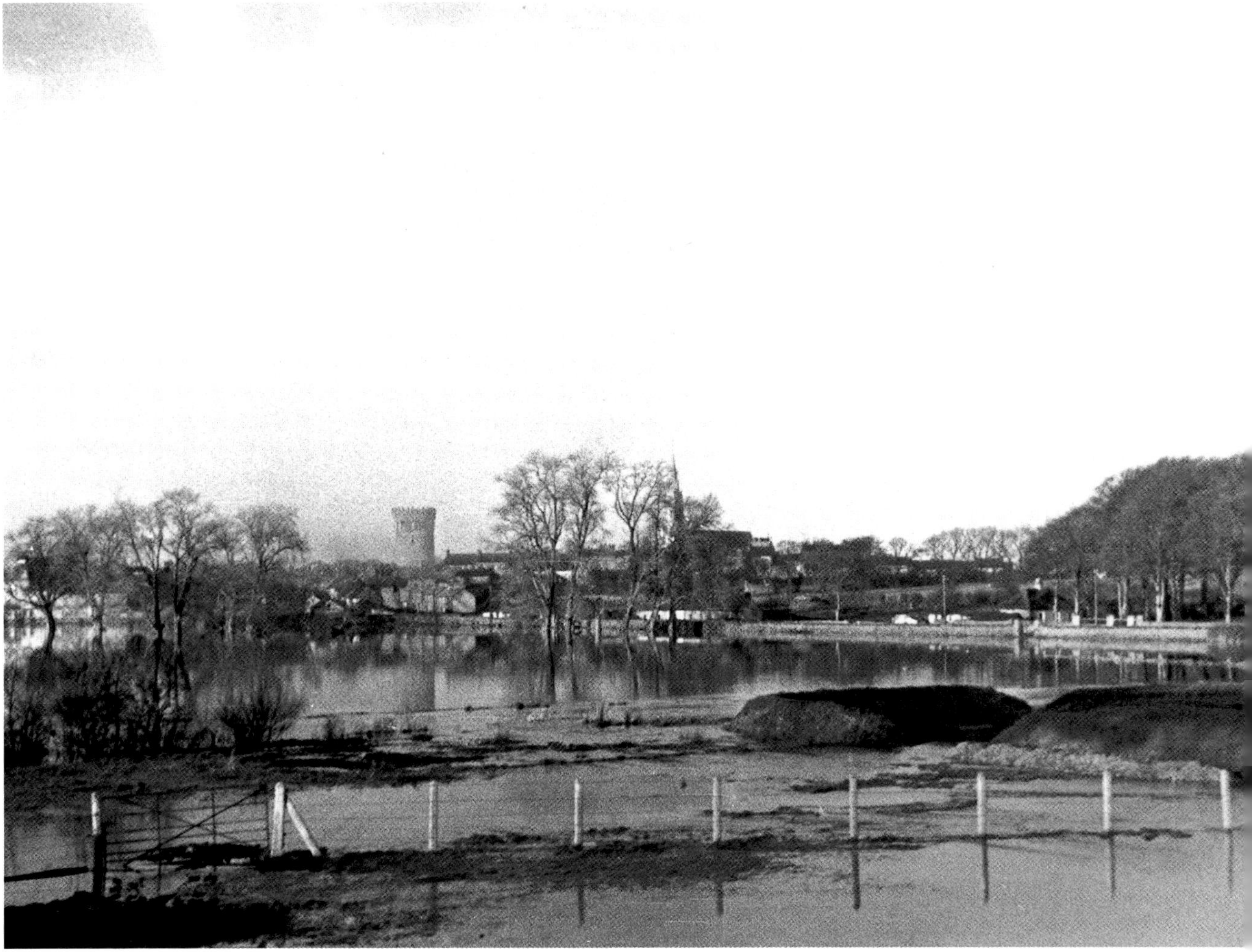

Floods at Nenagh (1938). The Nenagh and Ballintotty Rivers had both burst their banks.

Opposite page: Weir on the River Suir at Cahir. The railway bridge and the Church of Ireland steeple can be seen in the background (1942).

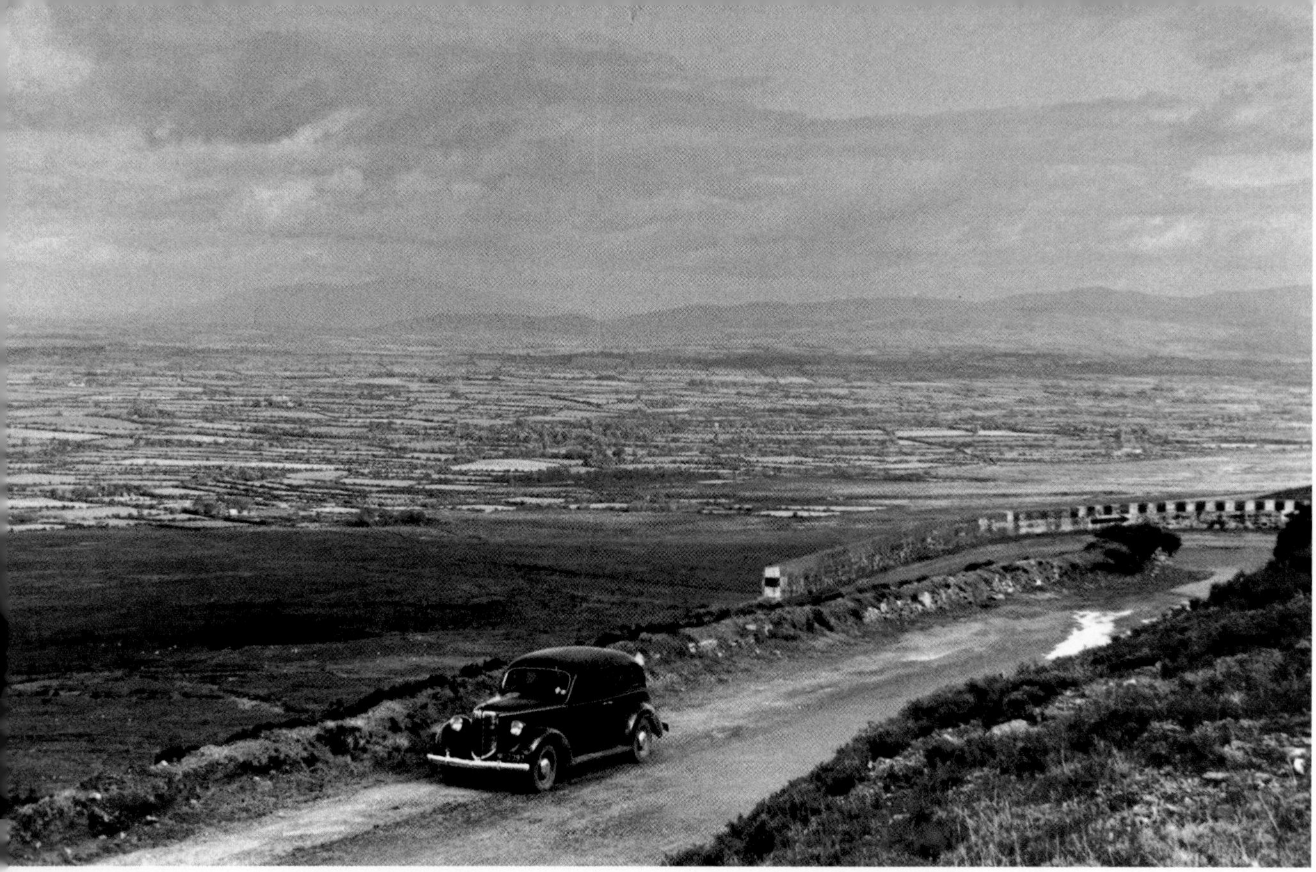

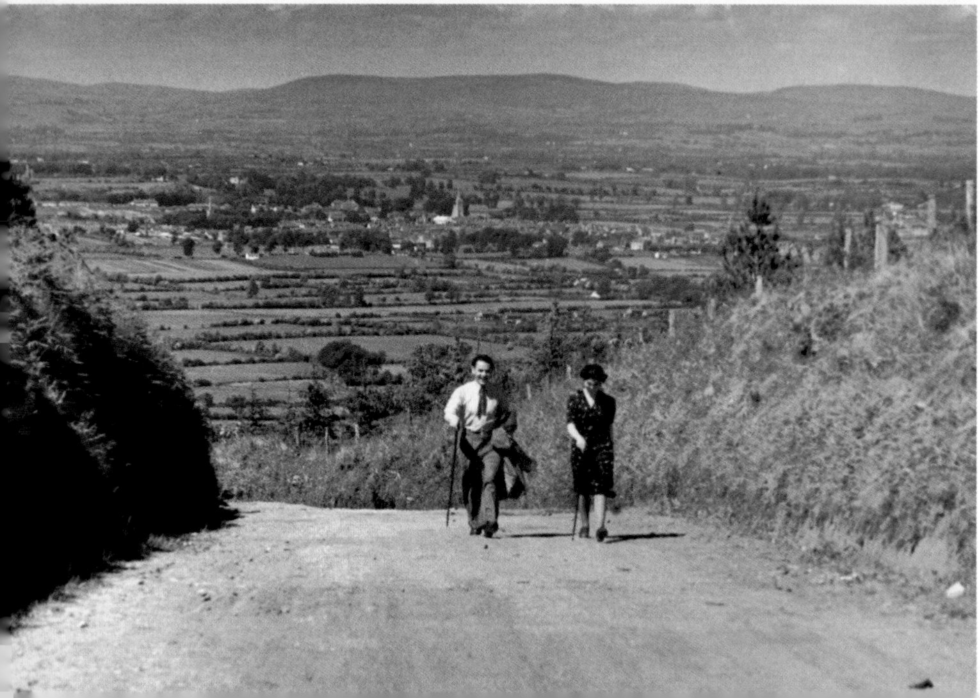

Above: 'The Vee' (1942). Taken above Clogheen on the road from Cahir to Lismore in the Knockmealdown Mountains.

Left: The Glen of Aherlow, taken from the rise above Lisvarrinane (1940).